Elisabetta Cirillo

NEW YORK CURIOUS

Illustrations by Monica Lovati

RIZZOLI
UNIVERSE

Contents

AMERICAN EXPRESS
PAUL VIONELLI

UNIONE EUROPEA
REPUBBLICA ITALIANA
PASSAPORTO

05:00

MetroCard

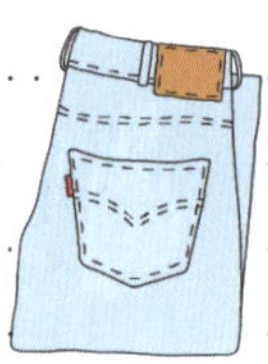

NARS
NARS

HABITS, CUSTOMS, QUIRKS & OBSESSIONS

bumble

NEW YORK ON FOOT

RAMBO

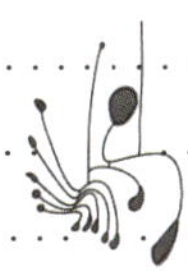

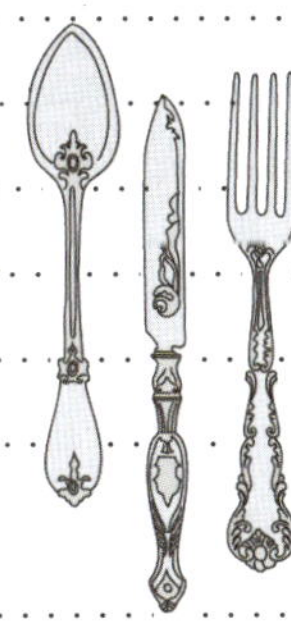

RIZZOLI

MANHATTAN BY NEIGHBORHOOD

BROOKLYN

THE OTHER BOROUGHS

GETTING OUT OF NEW YORK CITY

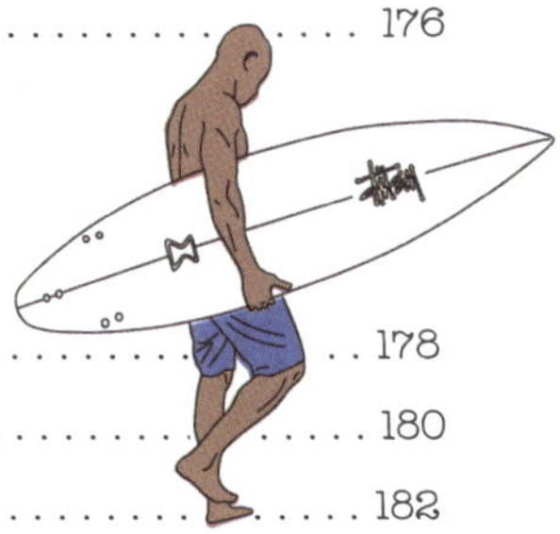

FOOD & DRINK

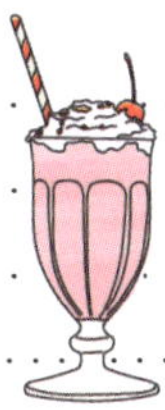

A YEAR IN NEW YORK

There was a time when New York was everything to me:
my mother, my mistress, my Mecca.

FROM *NIGHTS IN THE GARDENS OF BROOKLYN*

(HARVEY SWADOS

Somewhere deep in the belly of the city of New York, beneath the dark subsoil rooted in the Atlantic Ocean bed, there must be a gigantic, hidden magnet. What else could explain the pull the city has exerted for four centuries since 1624, drawing the world into its orbit? Its bold, bewitching mix of languages, nationalities, and cultures makes this metropolis an endless catalog of humanity.

Those who, like it or not, remain inescapably drawn to the city are called New Yorkers, but it is rarely because their roots are here, as you will discover. New Yorkers are a race apart. They are the people, in their white sneakers and outfits that waft a faint scent of laundry detergent, who leave their homes when the morning sun has just barely cleared the jagged Brooklyn skyline.

They are the people who strain every sinew and summon all their willpower to "make it here" (because, to paraphrase the song, then they can "make it anywhere"). The people who appear to thread their way as effortlessly as creatures in their natural habitat between cabs, sidewalks, steaming manhole covers, heel-grabbing gratings, packed railroad cars, and harried commuters.

The people who bolt down a bite to eat on a tiny patch of green squeezed between two skyscrapers that only here could be dignified with the name park or community garden, as composed as if they were dining at the Ritz, and who then, as evening falls, do battle with a sea of traffic and call an Uber to get to a place that has just opened halfway down some nameless backstreet in Queens. They take snaps of food that looks both exotic and indigestible, in a digital deluge of Instagram feeds that are the envy of the world.

New York City is the tough, hard-bitten capital of business, fashion, money, and vanity, and yet, in the cracks in the concrete, poetry can be found. Delve into its most secret corners and it will reveal itself to you in the most unexpected moments: in the last rays of a sunset filtered between apartment blocks, in pooled puddles of water reflecting traffic lights after a storm, in old streets that look as if they have sprung, fully formed, from a Hopper painting, and in the spirit of a city laid bare in a rare moment of silence on the ancient Red Hook pier, the Statue of Liberty looming in the distance.

It really is of no consequence that the sun may have set on one's Age of Innocence (Edith Wharton set her novel here). The beating heart of New York still pumps out jets of eternally renewable life. When asked what was so good about all this, Walt Whitman, another New Yorker to his very bones, responded in verse: "That you are here—that life exists and identity/ That the powerful play goes on."

Everyone can carve out a role for themselves in this powerful play. The Big Apple, however full of wonder and pulp, is within the reach of all; you just have to reach out and grab a little piece of it for yourself. In the hundreds of topics covered in this book, you will be taken to the places New Yorkers go, and witness their habits and quirks: how they don't look one another in the eye on public transit, the perpetual rush that they seem to be in, their eagerness to be the first to try an experience, their efficiency sometimes mistaken for abruptness, their passion for anything and everything different.

At the end of this exciting journey, you will know a little more about them, be a little less annoyed at them, and maybe even love them a little more. New Yorkers are not born; they are made, or rather the title is earned, like a medal for valor pinned to your chest with pride, despite all the scars. By reading this book, you might even be able to practice becoming one yourself.

Central Park
Subway
Lincoln Tunnel
TIMES SQUARE
MOMA
Hudson River
JACOBS
Levi's
SOHO
MIDTOWN
Welcome to
Little Italy
9A
CHINATOWN
East River
Williamsburg Bridge
Brooklyn Bridge
Manhattan Bridge
DUMBO
278

278

WHERE TO STAY

ASTORIA

Your choice of base will depend on your tastes and proposed budget, but it is worth taking certain factors into account, such as proximity to the subway, the safety of the area, and the distance from the places you plan to visit.

Queensboro Bridge

25

495

Due to its central and well-connected location, Times Square, for example, is a tourist favorite, but the area is extremely busy and full of noise

.

My advice?
Bear the rest of Midtown in mind too. It is just as well connected but a lot quieter.

If you want to save a few dollars, consider staying in other neighborhoods. Dumbo (in Brooklyn) and Astoria (in Queens) are both residential areas that are located a few stops from Manhattan.

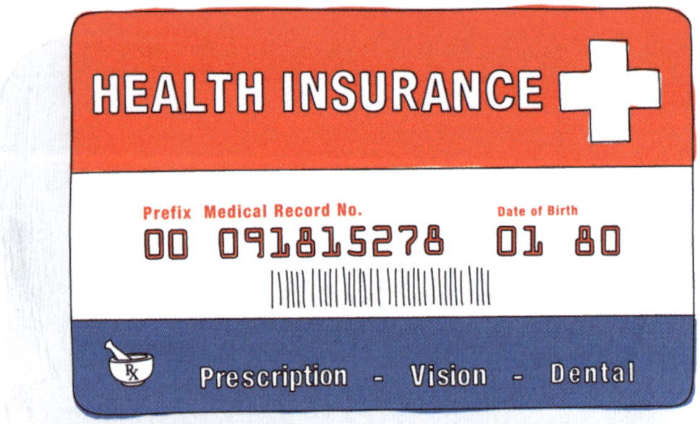

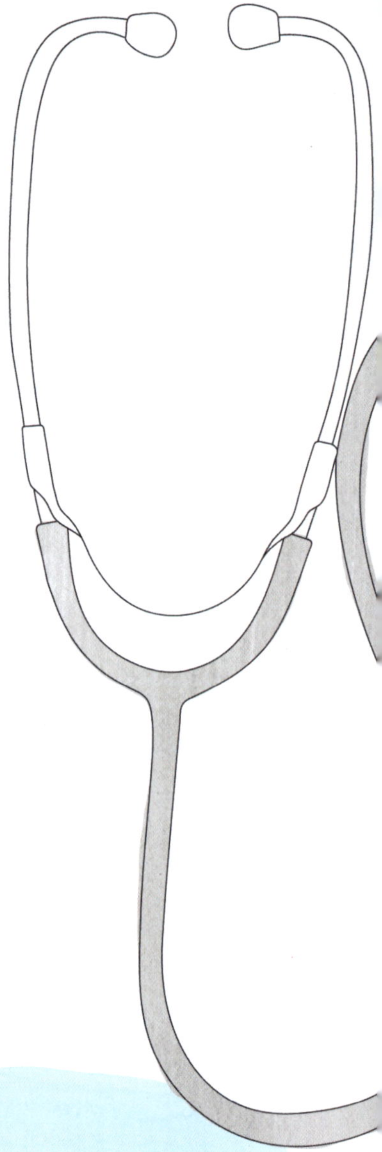

BEFORE YOU GO

HEALTH INSURANCE

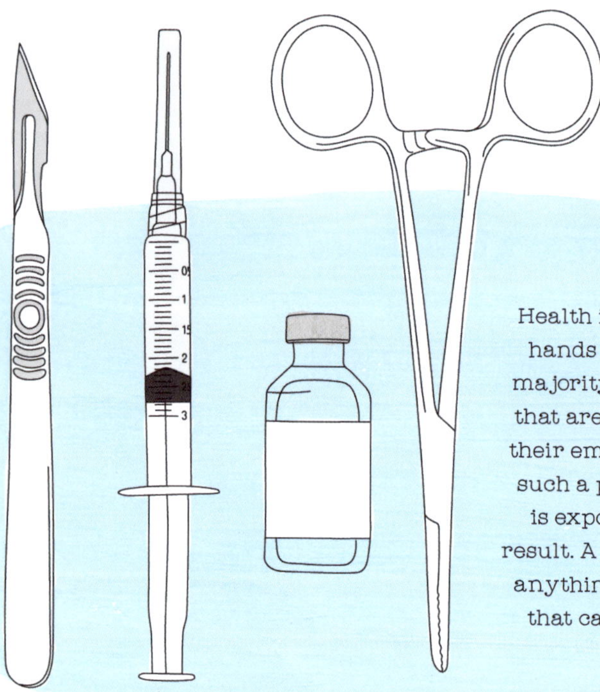

Health insurance is mostly in private hands in the United States, with the majority of citizens paying premiums that are then partially reimbursed by their employer. Anyone not covered by such a policy, which includes tourists, is exposed to considerable risk as a result. A simple appendectomy can cost anything up to $30,000 dollars, a sum that can rise to $85,000 for a traffic accident injury.

COLUMBUS
ASSICURAZIONI

columbusdirect.com

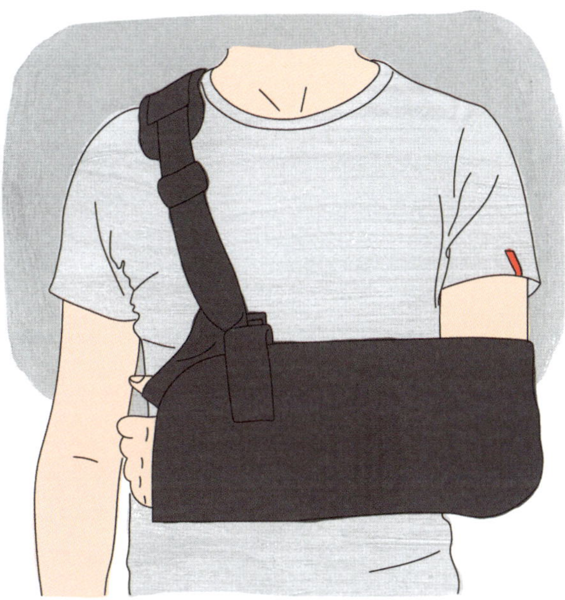

I would strongly advise taking out insurance before leaving home and ensure it provides adequate cover for the duration of your trip.

Allianz
Global Assistance

allianztravelinsurance.com

You can do this through your travel agent or online, if you have organized everything yourself.

europ assistance
you live we care

europ-assistance.com

BEFORE YOU GO

WHAT TO PACK

My advice would be to bring the absolute essentials and buy everything else when you get to New York. Comfortable shoes are an absolute must as NYC is the kind of city where you can easily walk 5–6 miles (10 km) in a day. The dress code is casual, and you can go almost anywhere in a pair of skinny jeans, sneakers, and a blazer and still look cool.

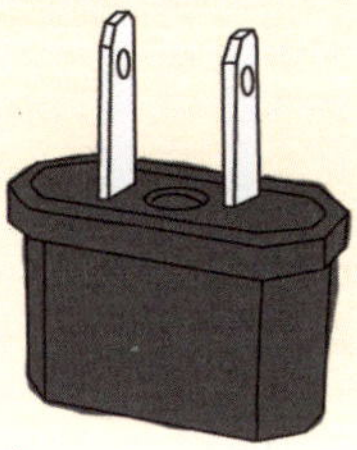

Don't forget a suitable plug adaptor for electricals and an ID document to supplement your passport, which is best left at your hotel for safety reasons. Keep this ID with you, as you will be asked to show it fairly often, especially in bars.

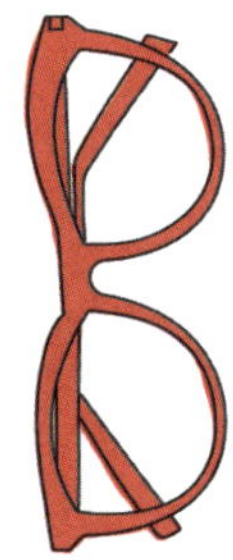

Maybe it is because the lights in Times Square are never turned off, but once you get to NYC, you'll find you simply have to buy certain things! Whatever your passion might be (sports, fashion, technology, or vintage clothes, you name it), the city has every conceivable option.

New York is the Mecca of marketing, after all!

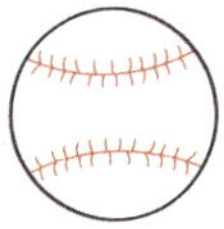

BEFORE YOU GO

CHANGING CURRENCY

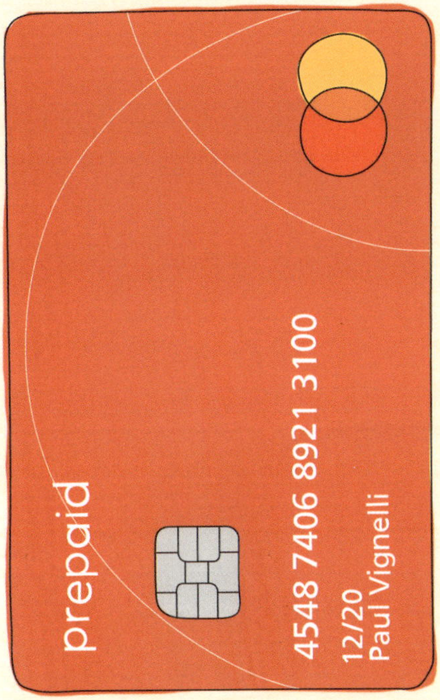

You can change currency directly at your bank branch before travel.

Don't forget, however, that you can buy almost anything with a credit card in NYC (even just a coffee), as well as use your phone to pay.

Buy a card-holder to attach to your cell phone, put your ID and prepaid card in it, and forget about cash!

CONNECTIVITY

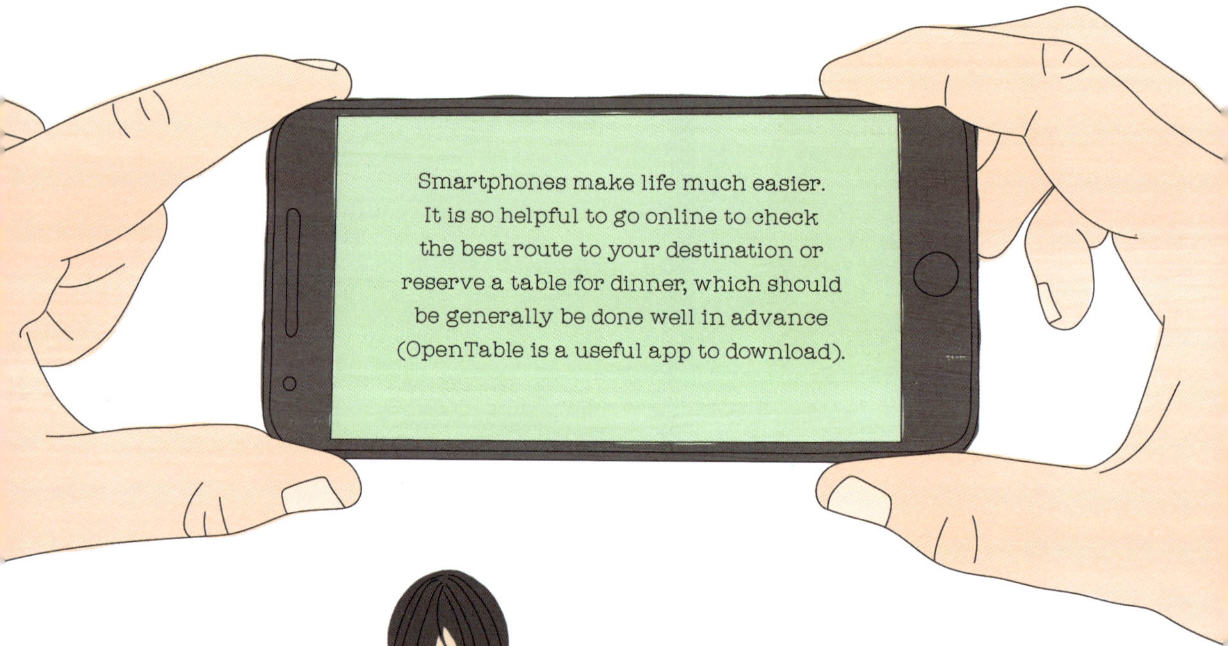

Finding free Wi-Fi is usually fairly easy in almost any bar and restaurant in New York, in shopping malls, and even on the subway. There are also special kiosks on the sidewalks where you can charge your phone battery and connect to the internet.

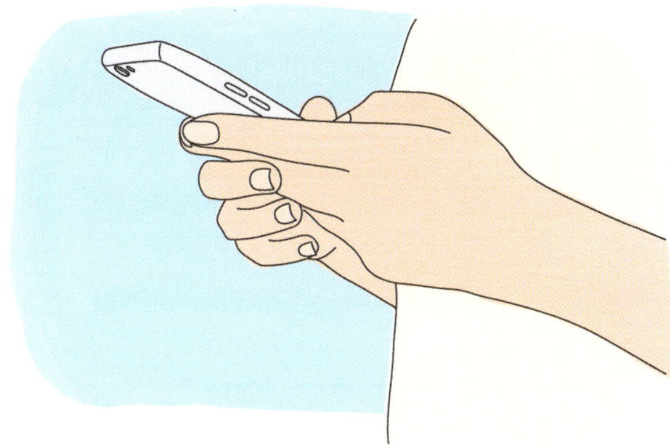

New Yorkers see their cell phone as an extension of their body, so you will be able to charge the battery in public places. Just ask.

One good option is to buy a local data plan as soon as you arrive. Most cell phone providers offer tourist plans for two weeks that guarantee unlimited internet access.

NETWORKING

MANHATTAN
FIELD NOTES
Put your connections to work! There's no shame in asking.

Before you leave, do some research and ask your friends and colleagues if they know anyone living in New York. You can put out feelers in the usual way, but social media can also be extremely useful.

Most ex-pats are delighted to share their insider's take on New York, but it is not advisable to meet up with someone you don't know on your own. Ideally, take a traveling companion with you.

WELCOME TO NYC

One of the most famous sayings associated with New York comes from the song immortalized by Liza Minnelli and Frank Sinatra: "If I can make it there, I'll make it anywhere."

There is plenty of evidence to suggest this is the case. Not only is the cost of living significantly higher, but vacations are half the length and working hours much longer than in many other countries. Giving it all you've got is sometimes not quite enough in New York.

That's why people say there's always a reason to be here. Are you following your dream? Are you achieving a goal you have set yourself?

This city is a vast playground, but it is also a giant pressure cooker in which it is a challenge to survive without having what are known in cities as "street smarts," the instinct that gets you out of trouble in any situation.

SURVIVING THE TIME DIFFERENCE

The time difference between most of Europe and the state of New York is six hours (five hours for the UK). When it's 6 P.M. in NYC, your body will feel as if it is already midnight, so for the first few days, you are likely to fall asleep early and wake up at the crack of dawn.

My advice for the first evening is to knock back a coffee and dive head first into the chaos of the metropolis. Take a nap if you must, but then head out to dinner and try to make it through until 10 P.M.

Chamomile

Valerian

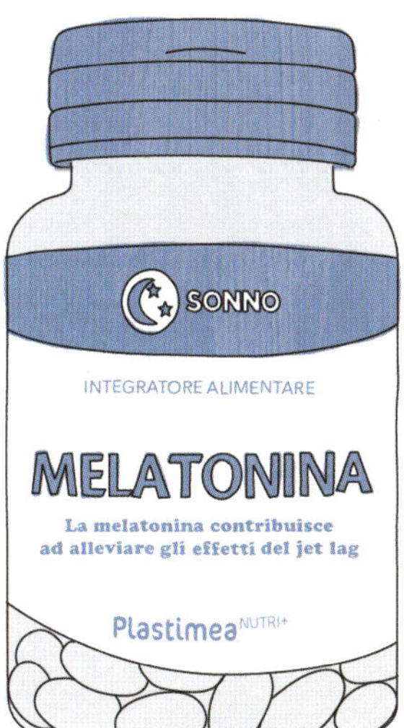

You are likely to wake up very early and find it hard to get back to sleep. Natural remedies like melatonin (prescription only in Europe) or a relaxing herbal tea can help with this.

GOOD TO KNOW

SURRENDER TO THE TIME ZONE

It is 5 A.M. and you are absolutely, positively, wide awake. Most stores won't be open until after 10 A.M., so what are you going to do, given that you can forget about the subway or a taxi until 9 A.M. because of the traffic?

Find the nearest diner and discover the wonders of breakfast in America!

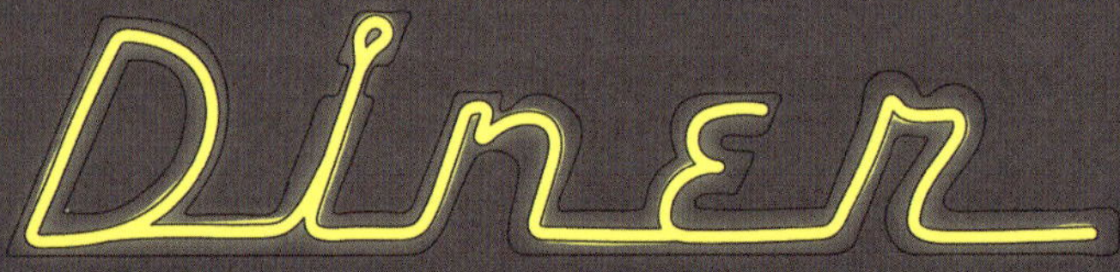

What exactly is a diner? It's that place just around the corner serving typical American food, with breakfast available at almost any hour of the day and a distinctly relaxed atmosphere.

ClassPass

If you are sporty, specialized apps (such as ClassPass) will let you book yoga, boxing, and gym classes in a flash. Alternatively, there is always the option of jogging in Central Park! The Big Apple might be the city that never sleeps, but be patient as it may take you a bit longer to adjust to its rhythms.

DOS & DON'TS

YES

Walk at a good pace to avoid slowing down the locals. This is Rule Number One. New Yorkers are renowned for being grumpy, a reputation that is (almost entirely) undeserved, but if you want to find out for yourself, just get in the way of a worker on their way into the office.

YES

Smile! People in NYC are inquisitive and, like anybody else, they love people-watching, but remember that we are the people they are watching, so smile and be open!

YES

Feel free to ask for directions, but be quick and efficient about it (see Rule Number One).

NO

To be cool, do what New Yorkers do: if you run into a celebrity, feign indifference!

NO

New York is a **veritable** melting pot of different cultures. Don't ask people where they are from; instead ask about their heritage in order not to cause any offence.

NO

Don't forget to leave a tip, or there'll be trouble! It will already be included on the check in some places (choose between 15, 18, 20, or 25 percent, depending on how you rate the service). If it's not included, it's wise to leave a minimum of 15 to 20 percent of the total. A tip of 20 percent is the norm in NY.

GOOD TO KNOW

GETTING AROUND WITH A CARD & PASS

First, buy a weekly pass for museums and public transportation. You will be making a small saving this way. There are several options on offer and you can compare them online and make your choice depending on planned activities. The most popular are the New York Pass, New York City Pass, and New York City Explorer Pass.

Subway

New York City Transit

Getting around on the subway will be easier with a MetroCard or OMNY card (One Metro New York), which you can buy at any station, plus the cost of whichever travel pass you want to get.

Important: Make sure you don't mix up Local subway lines, which stop at every station, with Express lines, which only serve the main stops.

All trains

If you have a smartphone, you can download apps such as Uber, Lyft, Curb, or Arro, which will come in handy during rush hour, when finding a cab can prove challenging.

NYC TAXI

citi bike

Another alternative is to use the bike-sharing service Citi Bike. Bear in mind that once you have rented a bike, you should swap it every 30 minutes to avoid paying a surcharge for extra minutes, but that shouldn't be a problem as there are loads of docks (more than 2,000 across the city). You can find a map of cycle paths at nycbikemaps.com.

GOOD TO KNOW

USEFUL PHRASES

New Yorkers are accustomed to a wide range of accents and levels of English, so there's no need to feel self-conscious. Don't hesitate to speak up, and if you don't understand, ask them to repeat themselves. The polite way to ask is:

"CAN YOU PLEASE SAY THAT AGAIN?"

A useful site to look at for slang expressions is UrbanDictionary.com (especially for the Yiddish* ones still in use).

* The language spoken by the majority of Jews in Central and Eastern Europe, including those who emigrated to the United States of America.

URBAN VOCABULARY

AKA: Acronym for "also known as."

ASAP: Acronym for "as soon as possible."

A SINGLE: A dollar.

ETA: Acronym for "estimated time of arrival."

KICKS: Sneakers.

SCHMEAR: A Yiddish word meaning cream cheese or other spread (usually in the phrase "a bagel with schmear," meaning a bagel with cream cheese).

STOOP: The flight of steps commonly found in front of New York houses.

TRAIN: Another name for the subway.

URBAN EXPRESSIONS

CAN YOU BREAK ME A HUNDRED?
Can you change a 100-dollar bill?

HAVE A GOOD ONE
Goodbye, farewell

IN A NEW YORK MINUTE
Very quickly

TAKE A RAIN CHECK
Postpone something
(This expression comes from the coupon issued for readmission to the replay of a baseball game that has been cancelled due to rain.)

SEEING IS BELIEVING

You will have no doubt seen the streets of New York in movies and television series, but once you're there in person, you'll realize that special effects are not involved! There really are puffs of white steam escaping from the manholes scattered throughout the city.

What's the reason for this phenomenon? It is related to the district heating system, which involved the distribution of superheated water through a network of underground pipes. This has protected NYC from the cold for more than a century. The steam is just very hot water vapor leaking out of cracks in the pipes or condensation brought about by abrupt changes in temperature.

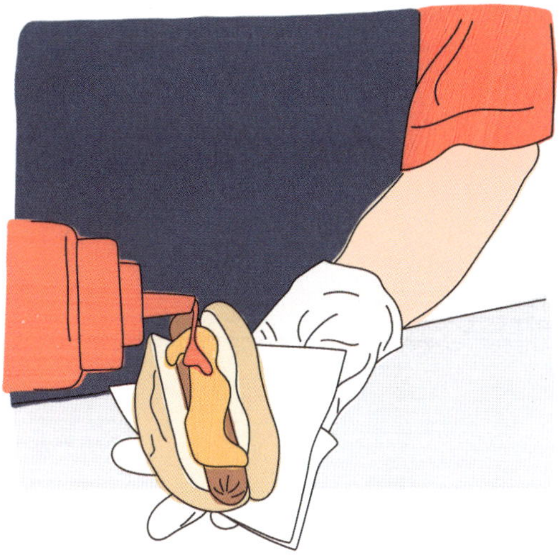

One of New York's highest population categories is, in fact, the humble rat! The problem has become increasingly acute in recent years, thanks to a constant rise in temperatures and a series of milder winters. So, if you happen to bump into a sewer rat on the street or in the subway, don't panic! Just continue on your merry way like a true New Yorker.

The roving food trucks you see everywhere were originally created to sell hot dogs and pretzels but now offer many other cuisines, including Mexican and Middle Eastern.

Food trucks are a popular option for a quick and cheap lunch for many New York workers, so much so that you will often see long lines of all kinds of people in front of them, not least businessmen in suits and ties.

GOOD TO KNOW

WHAT TO PACK TO BLEND IN

Everyone knows the essentials needed for a trip (sweater, hand sanitizer, travel card, pass, wet wipes, ID, etc.), but what are the cool and trendy folk sporting in NYC?

Tote bag

A simple canvas bag, perhaps purchased from, or given away by, your favorite store, is a must-have. It will come in handy for impulse purchases or as a smart alternative for an umbrella.

Headphones

A pair of headphones is an essential accessory for walking thirty blocks across Manhattan listening to cool sounds!

Water bottle

A metal or glass water holder (reusable and customizable) is vital. New Yorkers are paying increasing attention to things that are environmentally friendly and recyclable.

A DAY IN THE LIFE OF A NEW YORKER

Out of bed, get set, go! New York wakes up in waves and the longer the commuting distance (many workers will be coming from far-off areas like Brooklyn, or even New Jersey and Connecticut), the earlier you are forced to get up and embark on a journey of anything up to three hours.

The luckiest folk are those living in Manhattan, as their journey to work should take about 20 to 40 minutes on average. Most offices have a communal area where you can drink coffee and eat donuts. In New York, these sweet fried pastries covered in frosting are regarded as breakfast staples.

By the time 6 P.M. rolls around, the average New Yorker has spent at least an hour crammed into public transportation, had close encounters of an unpleasant kind with cockroaches, nasty odors, and odd people, and been confined to a cubicle for eight hours in front of a computer, all before returning to the tiniest apartment in the world.

This may be why happy hour is a foregone conclusion after a long day, and comes as a relief. In fact, it is often even organized by the offices themselves on a monthly basis to encourage socializing!

A DAY IN THE LIFE OF A TOURIST

Here are a few out-of-the-ordinary ideas for a city tour.

Irving Place, the street leading up to Gramercy Park (one of the two private parks reserved for local residents in the city, the other being Sunnyside Gardens Park in Queens), makes a very picturesque stroll, taking you back to a New York that was far more tranquil than today.

NEW YORK TRANSIT MUSEUM

If you hanker for evocative but almost forgotten places, head to City Hall Station, an old station built in a neo-Romantic style, which opened its doors in 1904 as the terminus of the first underground subway line, but was then abandoned in 1945. You can go inside if you book well in advance (information is available on the New York Transit Museum's website).

Take a ferry to admire New York from a wholly new angle for just a few dollars.

There are plenty of possible routes on the ferry.nyc website. Where you go isn't even that important, as just being on board and enjoying the view is an absolutely fascinating experience. The return trip from the southernmost tip of Manhattan to Staten Island is perfect for this.

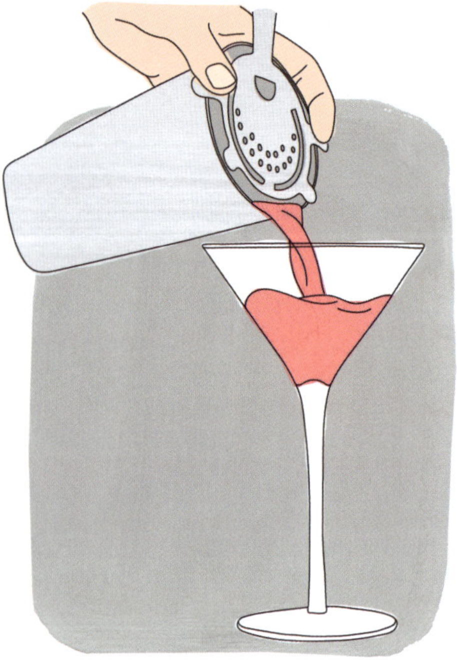

GOOD TO KNOW

A TYPICAL EVENING IN NEW YORK

It's Saturday evening, so what's the plan?

People often meet up for a drink at around 9 P.M. in New York City, occasionally opting to skip dinner altogether.

Despite having had a tough day, the average New Yorker rarely goes straight home after work. There's always a private view at some contemporary art gallery, a cocktail on offer in a store, or the launch of a new restaurant in which they want to be seen.

A trip to the movies is always popular and may differ from an average cinema-going experience in Europe. Lots of movie theaters allow you to order a cocktail and food from the comfort of your own seat, which might well recline for extra comfort.

Bars and clubs are also an option, although you might find that the average age of your fellow customers is higher than expected.

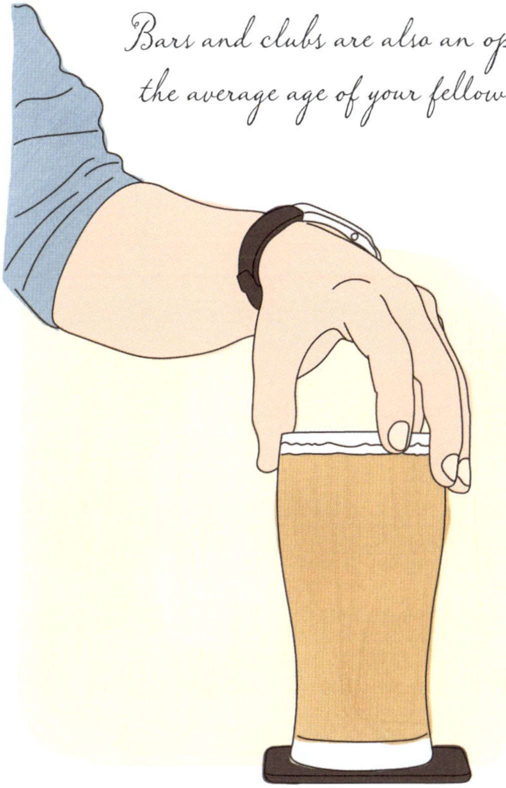

The most popular areas are the Meatpacking District, SoHo, and the Lower East Side. The nightclub scene takes off a bit earlier than in Europe, so heading to a venue at 11 P.M. is quite normal.

Club goers who emerge at dawn generally round the evening off with a slice of pizza at Artichoke or in one of the many Joe's Pizza outlets scattered across the city.

AN EVENING IN THE LIFE OF A TOURIST

If you're an art lover, don't forget that some museums are open later on Fridays and Saturdays (check out the websites of the Metropolitan, MoMA, and the Whitney), but don't expect to find them deserted as lots of people take advantage of the extended opening hours and potentially cheaper ticket prices. It's definitely a different experience, even if you have to stand in line for a while!

Instead of going for a classic Broadway show, consider something off-Broadway, where the shows are cheaper and sometimes more interesting.

There are a number of New York venues where you can enjoy dinner combined with an interactive experience, such as Ellen's Stardust Diner, where the cuisine is American, the servers are also singers, and the entire place is crammed with theater memorabilia.

MoMA: 1. *The Starry Night*, Vincent van Gogh; 2. *Bicycle Wheel*, Marcel Duchamp; 3. *Les Demoiselles d'Avignon*, Pablo Picasso.
Whitney Museum: 4. *Hanging Spider*, Alexander Calder; 5. *Green Coca-Cola Bottles*, Andy Warhol.
Met: 6. *Reclining Nude*, Amedeo Modigliani; 7. Arms and Armor Department.

SHOPPING: LUXURY GOODS

New York is an incredibly expensive city, so if there's one thing a true New Yorker can't resist, it's a bargain!

One of the city's most attractive initiatives is the "sample sale," a sort of private discount sale. Once you manage to get into your first one, I suggest you leave your email address at the door. That way, you'll definitely be admitted to the inner circle. But how do you go about finding that first one? Internet sites list them by product category, but you might also spot one as you are walking down the street.

Keep your eyes peeled!

There are also various outlet malls in NYC, including Nordstrom Rack Union Square, which has a very convenient central location and is fantastic for accessories, and Saks OFF 5TH if you want Saks quality but without their astronomical prices.

If you have the time and inclination to get out of the city, the best option is Woodbury Common Premium Outlets on the way to Albany in Upstate New York, a veritable temple of rock-bottom prices that can be reached by bus in 90 minutes from the Port Authority Bus Terminal.

GOOD TO KNOW

SHOPPING: FIND A BARGAIN

You can find real bargains at secondhand stores specializing in luxury brands, and there are plenty in SoHo. If purses are your thing, don't miss the store for the online platform The RealReal.

Vintage

Thrift shops are secondhand stores that offer an affordable alternative for vintage T-shirts and other items that are pretty rock'n'roll. L Train Vintage is one of the trendiest in town.

If you're looking to buy antiques, explore the flea markets. Brooklyn Flea and the Grand Bazaar NYC on the Upper West Side are a couple of the best known.

GOOD TO KNOW

SHOPPING: COOL STORES

As far as fashion is concerned, New Yorkers follow trends in both clothes and accessories, but they tend not to overdo it, instead pairing the latest trends with timeless pieces.

MISS CIRCLE NEW YORK

You will find bold and contemporary pieces in this trendy women's clothing boutique in the heart of SoHo. Perfect for anyone looking for cutting-edge fashion and a personal and creative shopping experience.

SUGAR COOKIES LINGERIE

An independent store in the heart of Manhattan's Chelsea neighborhood, founded by industry veteran Susanne Alvarado in 2008. This exclusive retailer is renowned for its tailored and personal approach to lingerie (available by appointment only).

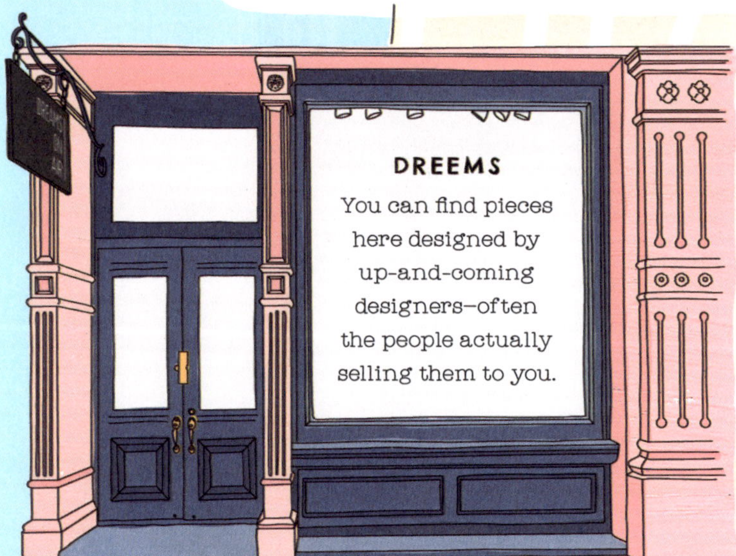

DREEMS

You can find pieces here designed by up-and-coming designers—often the people actually selling them to you.

Rizzoli

RIZZOLI BOOKSTORE

Founded by Angelo Rizzoli Sr in 1964 and located not far from Madison Square Garden, the Flatiron Building, and Eataly, the world's best bookstore for illustrated books on art, fashion, architecture, design, and photography is a must-visit.

FISH EDDY

Ceramics and glassware for the home, and very local.

ABC CARPET & HOME

You can find anything from homeware to children's toys in this store linked to the Jean-Georges restaurant chain.

East River

REFORMATION

The perfect spot for clothes that are super stylish, eco-friendly, and made in Los Angeles.

BEAUTY

There are plenty of small spas scattered across the city where you can drop in without an appointment. The most popular treatments are manicures, pedicures, and massages. If you are tempted by a foot massage after a long day on the hoof, don't forget to check the price list first.

Being curvy isn't a problem in New York, where personal style and confidence are always valued and admired.

Aesthetic perfection New York-style involves long eyelashes, well-groomed thick eyebrows, and long, pointed nails. Threading, an originally Middle Eastern depilatory technique that uses cotton thread to remove eyebrow hair, has become very fashionable.

Among the many and various temples to well-being (alongside the spas in the luxury hotels), you will find Aire Ancient Baths, a stunning thermal oasis built inside an old nineteenth-century factory in Tribeca.

Those who need forty winks between a stroll and a show should head for the recently opened Nap York in Midtown, a wellness center and sleep station where you can rest and recharge inside a special sleep pod.

GOOD TO KNOW

FITNESS

Fitness is a very different matter in New York compared to other parts of the world. Doing CrossFit might seem a bit obsessive to some, but in New York it's very much the norm.

Group classes are really popular, in particular the boot camp, where sessions are inspired by military techniques. You're guaranteed a ripped body as long as you can survive!

PRØJECT

Another recent craze among New Yorkers are fitness boutiques—small gyms that offer one or two kinds of workout and focus on building a community, which is especially popular with millennials. PROJECT by Equinox and Orangetheory Fitness are just two of those on offer.

If you are keen to work out without having to sign up for a membership, you can download apps such as ClassPass or Mindbody, which let you choose from different gyms and classes, and pay for lessons on an individual basis.

2 sets 10 repetitions
4 sets 10 repetitions
2 sets 5 repetitions
2 sets 5 repetitions
3 sets 10 repetitions

GOOD TO KNOW

SPORT

The main places to watch live sports in the evenings are the Yankee Stadium for baseball and Madison Square Garden or the Barclays Center for basketball, ice hockey, and boxing.

All sports have huge followings in New York, so going to see a local team play will be a unique experience, even if you're not much of a fan.

The US Open is one of the four Grand Slam tennis tournaments and has been held at Flushing Meadows-Corona Park in Queens from late August until the first couple of days in September since 1978.

The course of the New York City Marathon winds its way through all five boroughs. The event first took place in 1970 and now attracts more entrants than almost any other race. It is traditionally held on the first Sunday in November and you can always join the runners for a short stretch even if you haven't registered as a participant.

HABITS, CUSTOMS, QUIRKS & OBSESSIONS

HOW TO SPOT A NEW YORKER

Genuine New Yorkers are such rare birds that to be considered "from" the city, you don't need to be a scion of some local dynasty or Manhattan-born-and-bred. All it takes is to have lived in the Big Apple for ten years.

Characteristics of a New Yorker:

The Stereotype An air of suspicion toward everything, always dressed in black, disdainful of outsiders and tourists, rarely leaving their own neighborhood (especially in winter), and having a love/hate relationship with the city.

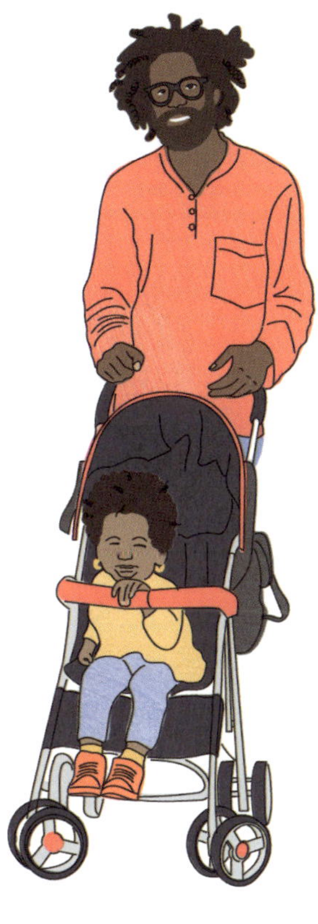

Characteristics of a New Yorker:

The Reality Unable to drive or cook, two skills that are practically superfluous in New York, but, importantly, very open-minded. New Yorkers are so unperturbed by weirdness that it is really difficult for anything to shock them.

A NEW YORK STATE OF OBSESSION

New Yorkers are like magpies, obsessed with new and shiny things.

Despite a certain degree of snobbishness, New Yorkers are willing to endure standing in endless lines to try the latest café. Blue Bottle Coffee was a case in point, as was the SugarFish restaurant, which opened in 2017. A cool new club attracts similar attention.

"OMG, you really have to go through the Lincoln Tunnel to get to work every day?"

Deli 24/7

New Yorkers' true obsession is efficiency. They want to get where they are going as quickly as possible. They despair if there isn't a deli within three blocks of their apartment. These bodegas are open 24/7 and sell the essentials, from toothbrushes to breakfast cereals and toilet paper. A subway station on the corner of your home street is a non-negotiable.

FAMOUS NEW YORKERS

New York is the birthplace of some of the most talented and influential people in the world, including Humphrey Bogart, Maria Callas, John D. Rockefeller, Al Capone, Stanley Kubrick, Theodore Roosevelt, Eleanor Roosevelt, and many more.

Theodore Roosevelt was the 26th president of the United States (from 1901 to 1909), and his face is carved into Mount Rushmore alongside George Washington, Thomas Jefferson, and Abraham Lincoln. The house where Roosevelt was born is now a national historic site and is the only presidential birthplace open to the public. It is located in the Flatiron District in Manhattan.

A few bars where New York celebrities have been known to meet in the past:

The White Horse Tavern was opened in 1880 as a place for dockworkers to relax after their shift but, from the 1950s, it became a rendezvous for writers and artists, from Dylan Thomas to Bob Dylan and Jack Kerouac.

PJ Clarke's opened as a saloon in 1885 and was a favorite haunt of both Frank Sinatra, who always sat at table 20, and the actor Richard Harris, who would order "the usual," which tended to be a good six double vodkas. They still serve some of the best burgers in the city here.

If you are interested in celebrity spotting, there is a variety of websites (such as celebmap.com) where you can find the homes and most popular hangouts of the stars. You can also go on specialized guided tours that will take you to the iconic locations from your favorite movies and sitcoms.

HABITS, CUSTOMS, QUIRKS
& OBSESSIONS

LANGUAGES SPOKEN

The most commonly spoken languages in New York are English and Spanish, followed by East Asian languages (principally Chinese).

It has been estimated that some 800 languages (official and dialects) are spoken in the five boroughs. Among its other attributes, Queens is the place where the most languages are spoken in the world, and within just a few miles, you can hear everything from Greek to Filipino, Urdu, and Indonesian.

New York is truly the global capital of linguistic diversity.

Polyglot evening

There are lots of options available to those keen to learn a foreign language, including so-called polyglot evenings during which all you have to do is wear a badge showing the languages you know and those you'd like to practice. It is the perfect way to take advantage of New York's multiculturalism.

ACRONYMS & ABBREVIATIONS

Most of the neighborhoods in NYC have an acronym or abbreviation by which they are affectionately known by locals. Here are a some examples:

UES
UPPER EAST SIDE

UWS
UPPER WEST SIDE

TRIBECA
TRIANGLE BELOW CANAL STREET

LES
LOWER EAST SIDE

FIDI
FINANCIAL DISTRICT

DUMBO

DOWN UNDER THE MANHATTAN BRIDGE OVERPASS

SOHO

SOUTH OF HOUSTON* STREET

NOHO

NORTH OF HOUSTON* STREET

Nolita

NORTH OF LITTLE ITALY

Nomad

NORTH OF MADISON SQUARE PARK

* An infallible way of telling a tourist from a local is in the correct pronunciation of this street which divides the southern part of Manhattan in two: New Yorkers pronounce the first syllable as "how" (to rhyme with "cow") and not as "Hugh," like the eponymous city in Texas.

CLASSES

Classes to take in your leisure time are one of the most frequently changing fashions in New York.

Barre class & heels dance

A few years ago, everyone was signing up for classes in zumba and barre (a half-ballet, half-aerobics workout), but the recent trend is for heels dance and any kind of activity that can be combined with a glass of wine. Whether you're creating pots, paintings, or pizzas, there will always be a nice drop of wine at your elbow.

A few interesting ways in which you can try to live like a true local include downloading an app like Meetup and joining groups that get together for different activities, or checking out the website CourseHorse, where you can browse a wide selection of courses.

Mommy & Me

So-called Mommy & Me classes are also popular, promoting interaction between children without siblings or without access to a garden to play in. Activities include anything from country music to painting, dancing, and yoga.

URBAN LEGENDS

The most famous New York urban legend is probably the one about crocodiles living in the sewers. Rumor has it that the underground infestation of these reptiles began when they were released by a child who had been keeping them as pets.

Another famous story is about the illuminated Pepsi-Cola sign in Queens.

Legend has it that the sign was built at the request of Joan Crawford, the famous actress and wife of a president of the Pepsi company. When she wanted to move into a building on the shores of Manhattan looking out over the East River, she was blackballed by the condominium residents' association (in New York these are called co-ops, whose approval is required in order to be able to buy an apartment), the chair of which was the CEO of Coca Cola. She retaliated by having the enormous sign erected, so her not-to-be neighbors wouldn't forget her or her husband's firm in a hurry.

Many of the stories revolve around ghosts.

The most infamous one involves the Dakota Building on the Upper West Side, famous not only for Roman Polanski's 1968 movie *Rosemary's Baby* (the exteriors were shot here) but also as John Lennon's last home (he was killed outside the building in 1980).

Interesting fact

The building's history goes back much further, however. It transpires that many of its owners have been fans of occultism and séances, to the extent that there have been numerous reported sightings of a ghost of a small girl over the years, and even of Lennon himself.

9/11 MEMORIAL

Memories of September 11, 2001, have not faded in New York. Many people lost someone that day, and everyone lost something.

Emotions run high each year when the families of the victims gather to lay red roses beside the pools where the names of the dead are engraved.

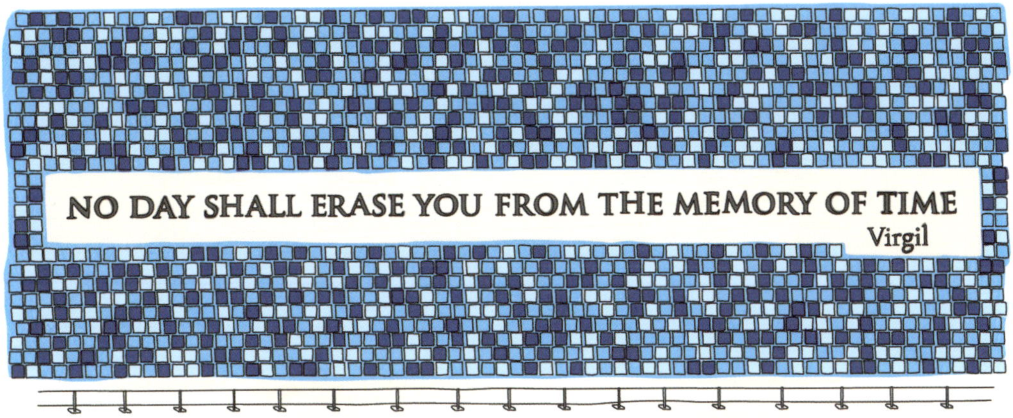

World Trade Center Transportation Hub

Designed by the architect Santiago Calatrava, the World Trade Center Transportation Hub (aka the Oculus) is a large subway station that also houses an extensive shopping mall.

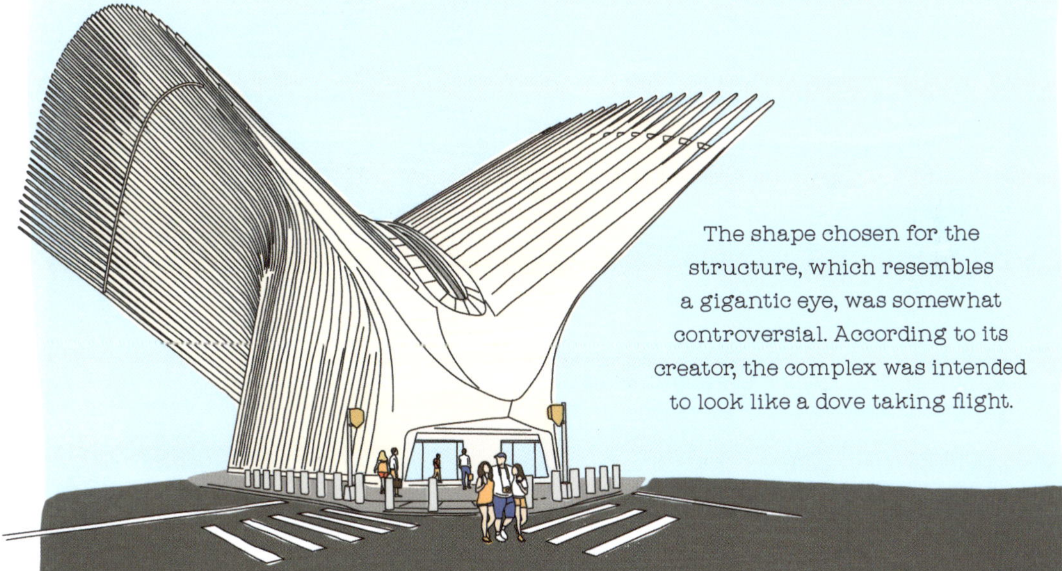

The shape chosen for the structure, which resembles a gigantic eye, was somewhat controversial. According to its creator, the complex was intended to look like a dove taking flight.

The Oculus divided the city and its spiraling cost (more than $4 billion) left most New Yorkers perplexed, but it soon became a very popular shopping destination.

HIGH-END NEW YORK

New York is home to 125 billionaires and has one of the highest numbers of so-called high-net-worth individuals of any city in the world. This means that there is far more extravagance here than elsewhere, and all kinds of services are flourishing, such as luxury concierge services that can deliver anything your heart might desire, from a private shopper to a personal organizer.

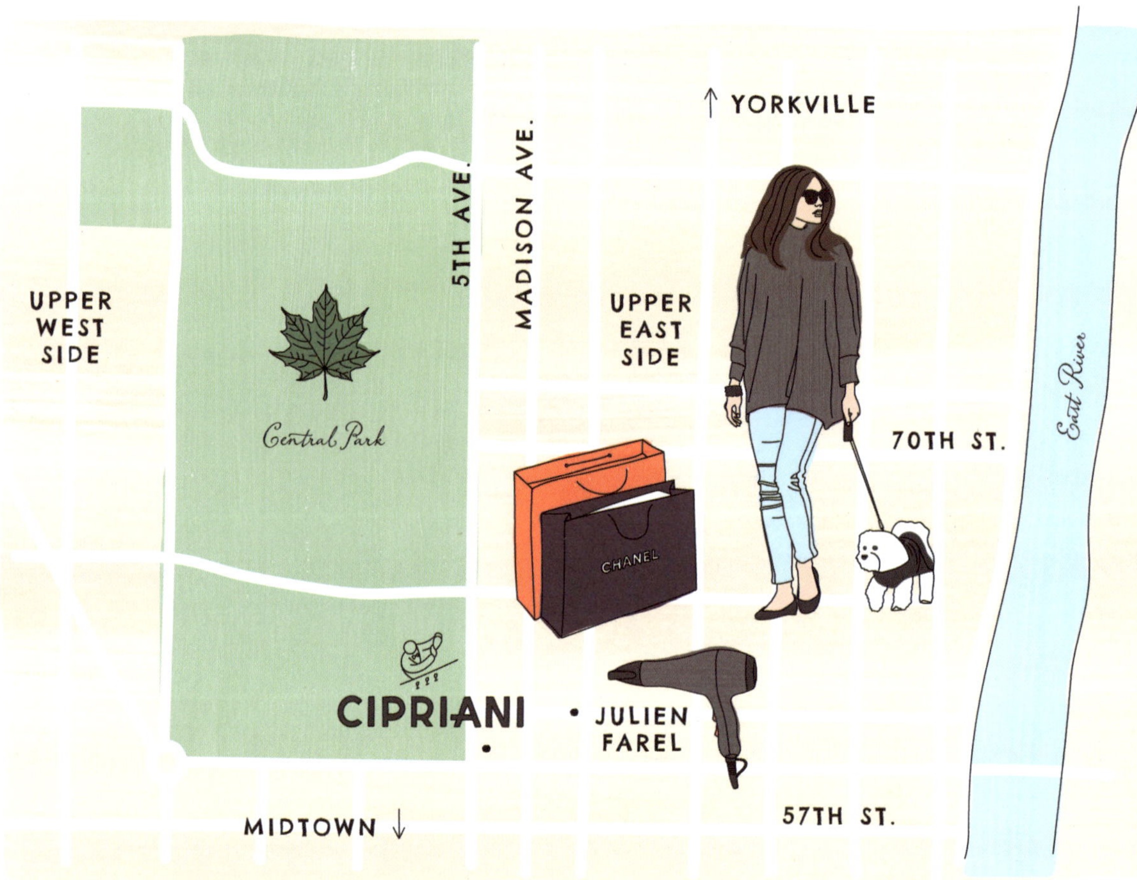

The most well-to-do part of Manhattan is undoubtedly the Upper East Side, in particular from 57th to 70th Street, between Madison Avenue and Fifth Avenue. It is here you are likely to see well-heeled ladies gathering at Cipriani, walking their small, white dogs and getting their hair done at Julien Farel's Restore Salon & Spa before rounding off their day with a browse in Hermès in Madison Avenue.

THE MET

The Met Gala, an exclusive social event held in the Metropolitan Museum in early May, draws the world's most influential celebrities. In order to get through the door, you must first secure an invitation and then shell out a huge sum ($75,000 in 2025). Note that this does not take into account the cost of your wardrobe, which must be inspired by the annual chosen theme.

SEX & THE CITY (1)

A brief introduction to the concept of dating

While in many countries romantic options are largely limited to being part of a couple or on the market, America recognizes an intermediate phase between the two, known as dating, which allows you to dodge the question. But don't confuse dating with a relationship: some New Yorkers are allergic to attachments.

Getting together

Since New York is such a diverse, tolerant, and multicultural city, there are many opportunities for single New Yorkers to meet new people and enjoy dating. It is a fantastic city for those looking for an exciting social life.

New York women are sassy, confident, and fashionable.

New York is perfect for fashionistas who enjoy dressing up and making an impression!

Anything goes in New York, so wear what you want, slip off your shoes, and have fun: no one will notice.

Hail a cab!

New Yorkers work hard, but they also like to play hard. They enjoy a good night out with friends, whether at the latest nightclub or the most fashionable bars. Having fun can go on late into the night, so many New Yorkers prefer to hail a cab to get home.

SEX & THE CITY (2)

It's getting increasingly difficult to meet new people in today's atomized society, even in an overpopulated city like New York, and this may explain why dating apps are much more popular here than in other countries.

bumble

One of the best-known dating apps is called Bumble, which is also available as variants like Bumble BFF to find new friends and Bumble Bizz for professional networking. And to go the extra mile, Bumble also organizes evenings for real-life, face-to-face introductions.

A typical location for a romantic tryst might be one of the bijou restaurants in Koreatown, a small area of Midtown squeezed between Madison Avenue and Sixth Avenue, around 32nd Street.

What makes these places special is that they generally serve meat cooked directly on a tabletop grill. You'll also find the venues are atmospheric and popular with locals.

LGBTQ+ NEW YORK

New York is an unprejudiced, gay-friendly city. The first Gay Pride march was held in Greenwich Village in 1969 and the neighborhood is considered the epicenter of the gay rights movement.

Stonewall Inn, 53 Christopher Street

If you want to discover more about the historic sites of the LGBTQ+ community, a good place to start is the area where the West Village meets Chelsea, before moving on to the neighborhoods that have become bastions of the community more recently (such as Hell's Kitchen, Williamsburg, and Queens).

At 159 West 10th Street you will find Julius, one of New York's first gay bars. It opened its doors in 1867 and the gay community has been coming in since 1950.

The Big Gay Ice Cream Shop was a beloved local landmark—a hip, convivial ice cream parlor known for its inventive soft-serve creations and its celebration of creativity and inclusion. It has since closed, but it remains fondly remembered.

TWO HISTORICAL SNAPSHOTS

The first European to reach the area where New York City now stands was the Italian Giovanni da Verrazzano in 1524.

In 1609, Henry Hudson sailed up the river that was later to bear his name.

The first attempts to establish a colony in New York were made by the Dutch in 1626, with Peter Minuit "purchasing" Manhattan from Native Americans for the modern equivalent of $24.

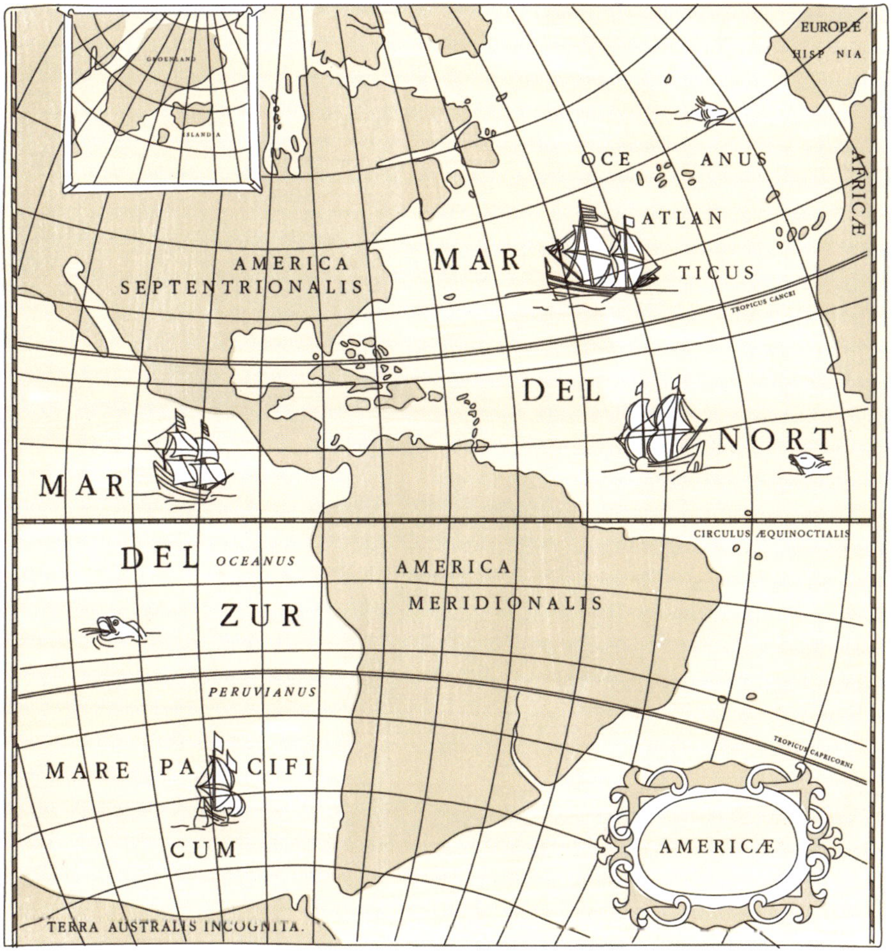

New York has continued to flourish, due in part to the many immigrants who have helped to shape its character and turn it into the city that, more than any other, embodies the hope of achieving the so-called American Dream.

NEW YORKERS' LOVE FOR WEIRD ACRONYMS

New Yorkers have an enduring obsession with finding new acronyms for various neighborhoods, and there has been a recent trend to coin new, sometimes rather surreal, names for increasingly specific areas. The oddest include:

BoCoCa

The area between Boerum Hill, Cobble Hill, and Carroll Gardens.

RAMBO

Stands for "Right After the Manhattan Bridge Overpass," an area next to Dumbo.

BAMBI

"Beyond Allen at the Manhattan Bridge Intersection,"
the southernmost extent of the Lower East Side.

REBECHA

"Rectangle Below Chambers refers to the parallelogram formed by Chambers Street, Broadway, Whitehall Street, and Water Street.

SpaHa

Spanish Harlem, the "Latino" part of a neighborhood mostly inhabited by African Americans.

Staten Island

The least-visited borough, especially by New Yorkers. The writer George R. R. Martin said in an interview that he took inspiration from Staten Island when imagining the map of Westeros, the western continent that is the setting for *A Song of Ice and Fire*, a saga on which the series *Game of Thrones* was based.

The Bronx

Everyone knows The Bronx by reputation, especially from movies like *The Warriors* (1979), but New Yorkers have always been aware that the borough also boasts the biggest zoo in New York, along with a splendid botanical garden and the Yankee Stadium. It was also the birthplace of hip-hop and is famous for its graffiti.

Queens

New York's second-most populous borough is also the most diverse, with the highest concentration of different nationalities. City dwellers flock here in increasing numbers to sample cuisines from around the world, with the most authentic restaurants you will find in the city.

Brooklyn

The most populated borough has undergone a sea change in recent years, gaining a reputation for a wide variety of events and activities, including concerts and sports fixtures, but in particular for its nightlife. The center of gravity is increasingly shifting from Manhattan because everything here is cool and underground, with secret brunches, members-only clubs, and new (and expensive) restaurants.

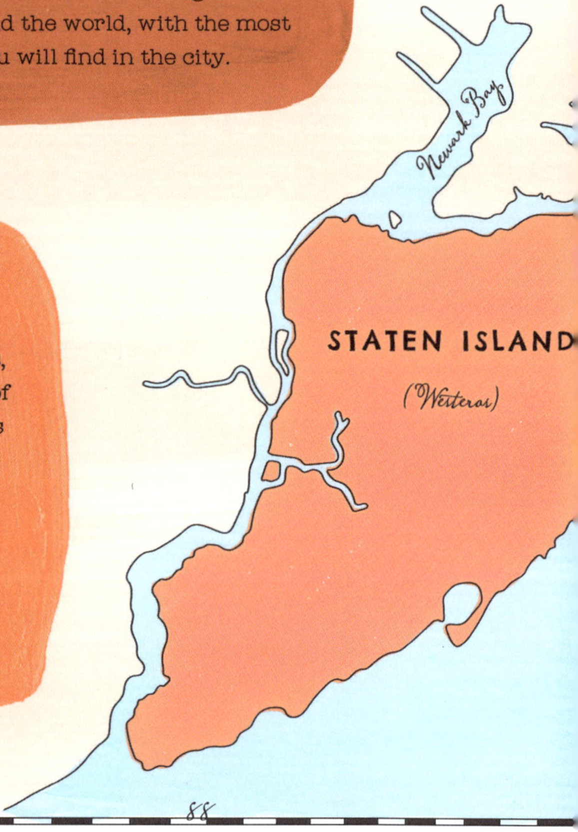

NEW YORK ON FOOT

A MAP OF THE BOROUGHS

Manhattan is the star of the show. The most densely populated borough also attracts the most tourists and is more closely identified with the City of New York than any other. It is the administrative, financial, and economic center of the metropolis, and the scene of some of the most significant events in its history. The island is divided into neighborhoods and, over the years, many of these have in turn been subdivided into smaller and sometimes very different areas, all of which are worth exploring.

NEW YORK ON FOOT

MANHATTAN

THE NEIGHBORHOOD

Residents of Manhattan are usually the ones considered true New Yorkers, partly because it has become increasingly rare to find long-term residents there.

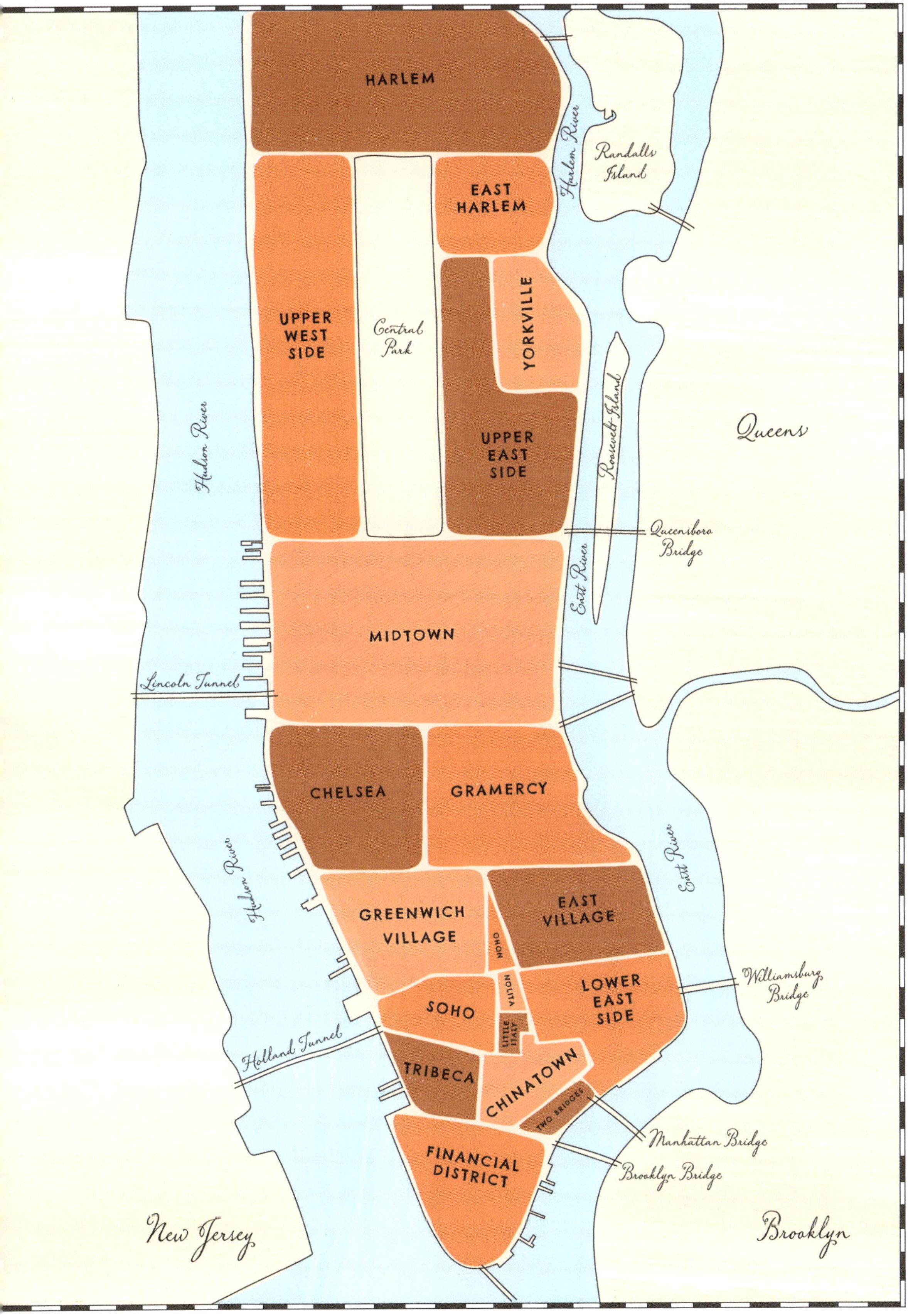

HARLEM
Harlem River
Randalls Island
EAST HARLEM
UPPER WEST SIDE
Central Park
YORKVILLE
Roosevelt Island
Queens
UPPER EAST SIDE
Hudson River
Queensboro Bridge
East River
MIDTOWN
Lincoln Tunnel
CHELSEA
GRAMERCY
Hudson River
East River
GREENWICH VILLAGE
EAST VILLAGE
NOHO
NOLITA
LOWER EAST SIDE
Williamsburg Bridge
SOHO
LITTLE ITALY
Holland Tunnel
TRIBECA
CHINATOWN
TWO BRIDGES
Manhattan Bridge
FINANCIAL DISTRICT
Brooklyn Bridge
New Jersey
Brooklyn

LANDMARKS: FAMOUS VIEWS

New Yorkers have a reputation for not being particularly fond of tourists and for shunning tourist traps, but even they find it difficult to resist the charms of places like the Brooklyn Bridge or avoid passing through stations such as Grand Central. Who could resist the comforting refuge of a green lung like Central Park when life in the metropolis becomes overwhelming?

You will see plenty of tourists on Brooklyn Bridge, but also lots of commuters on their way to work. Many are cyclists, so if you are using the bike lanes, respect the rules of the road or you risk having an irate New Yorker explaining them to you rather forcefully.

Grand Central is not just a major subway and railroad station, but also a very popular meeting spot for New Yorkers. Inside, you can play a couple of sets at the Vanderbilt Tennis Club, pick up some fresh produce at the Grand Central Market, or treat yourself to a seafood dinner at the renowned Grand Central Oyster Bar.

The *Charging Bull* sculpture in Wall Street was created by the Italian artist Arturo Di Modica in 1989. In 2017, a sculpture by the American artist Kristen Visbal entitled *Fearless Girl*, depicting a defiant-looking youngster, was placed in front of the bull, provoking instant outrage from Di Modica, who maintained that the second statue had radically changed the meaning of his own work.

A third artist then felt inspired to join the conversation by adding a third element to the composition, a dog caught in the moment of urinating on the *Fearless Girl*. Although this last statue was removed overnight, the bold girl, who was supposed to remain in place for just a few days as a publicity stunt, was moved and installed permanently in front of the NYC Stock Exchange, much to the delight of locals, who were very aware of the gender equality message it promoted.

MUSEUMS

The recently renovated Frick Collection is housed in a Beaux-Arts mansion that once belonged to the steel magnate Henry Clay Frick. It is located at 1 East 70th Street on the Upper East Side. In addition to its permanent collection, it hosts frequent temporary exhibitions. It's definitely worth a visit, if only to admire the building.

The Tenement Museum at 103 Orchard Street is listed as a national historic site. The building recreates the living conditions experienced by immigrants on the Lower East Side, historically the area inhabited by newcomers to Manhattan.

The museum organizes various guided tours, some even with actors. Checking the tenement.org website before planning your visit is always a good idea.

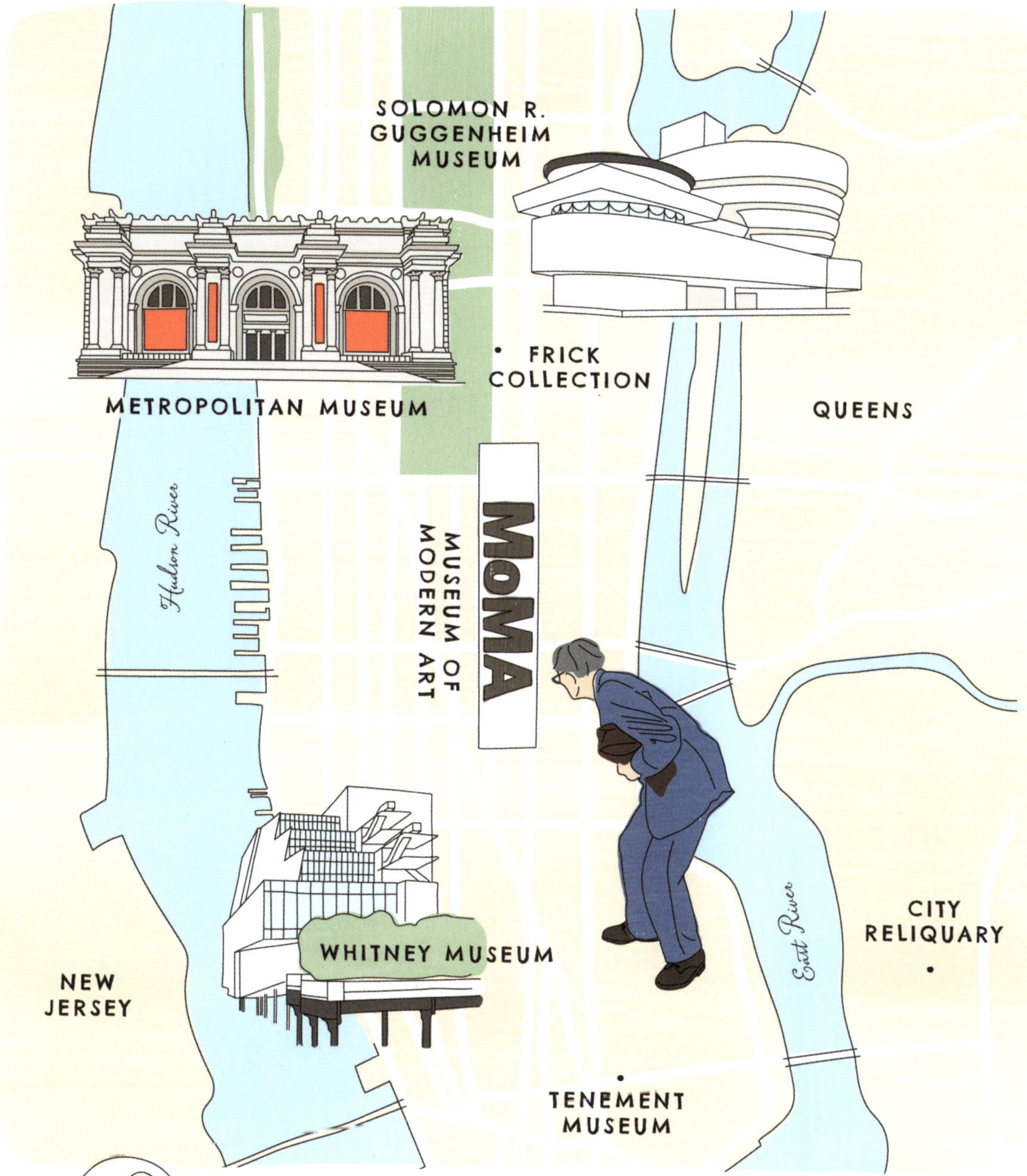

The City Reliquary is a small-scale, nonprofit "community museum" located in Williamsburg, Brooklyn, with a mission to share everyday items that have helped to make New York great over the years, from models of the Statue of Liberty to the rope that held the mourning drape after the attacks of September 11, 2001.

PARKS

Central Park is the biggest park in Manhattan and the most popular place for locals to exercise (with most runners gravitating toward the area around the reservoir). Have a summer picnic on Sheep Meadow, sunbathe, or take the kids out for a breath of fresh air.

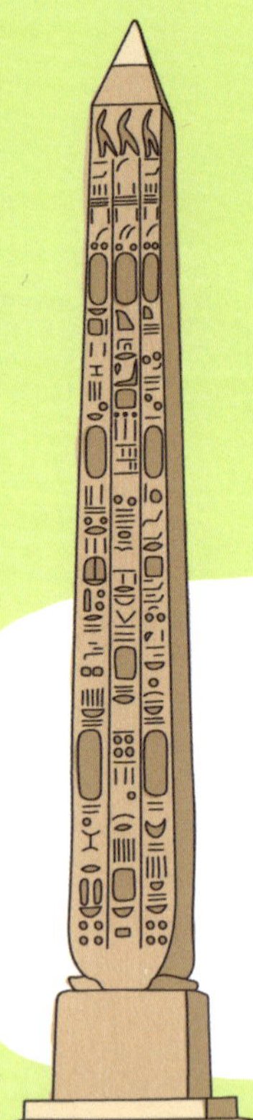

Cleopatra's Needle

The oldest object in Central Park is Cleopatra's Needle, an Egyptian obelisk from the fifteenth century BCE that was transported from Alexandria in Egypt to New York in 1880 by the philanthropist William Henry Vanderbilt.

Riverside Park

Riverside Park looks out over the Hudson River to the west of the city and has the most beautiful views in New York, according to many. In addition to being an ideal spot for a jog or a sunset stroll, it is home to a number of unexpected features, such as the Bird Sanctuary (between 116th and 124th Streets), where some 180 species of bird have been spotted over the last thirty years, and the Hamilton Fountain, one of the city's last surviving decorated horse troughs.

In addition to the classic parks, and the smaller ones such as Bryant Park and Washington Square Park, you should visit the New York Botanical Garden in the Bronx (the largest botanical garden in the city), or Brooklyn Botanic Garden, which is smaller but a more agreeable place for a pleasant stroll.

THEATERS

The Theater District, comprising about forty playhouses grouped together in a relatively small space, is one of the city's main attractions. Ticket prices are a bit higher than in Europe, but it's useful to know that tickets can be marked down by up to 50 percent on the day of the show. Check out the TDF Ticket Discount Booth, located underneath the flight of red steps on 47th Street and Broadway.

Off-Broadway

New Yorkers tend to prefer Off-Broadway shows, which are generally smaller-scale productions and often slightly off-the-wall, such as *Drunk Shakespeare*, in which professional actors knock back at least five shots of whiskey before going on stage and performing one of the Bard's great works.

If you visit New York in the summer months, take the opportunity to see a Shakespeare in the Park show in Central Park. Tickets are free, but be prepared to stand in a long line to secure them.

The Lincoln Center on the Upper West Side is a complex of buildings almost all of which are dedicated to the performing arts. You should try to see at least one show at the Metropolitan Opera House, even if you're not an opera buff or ballet aficionado. Some of the greatest productions in the world are performed here.

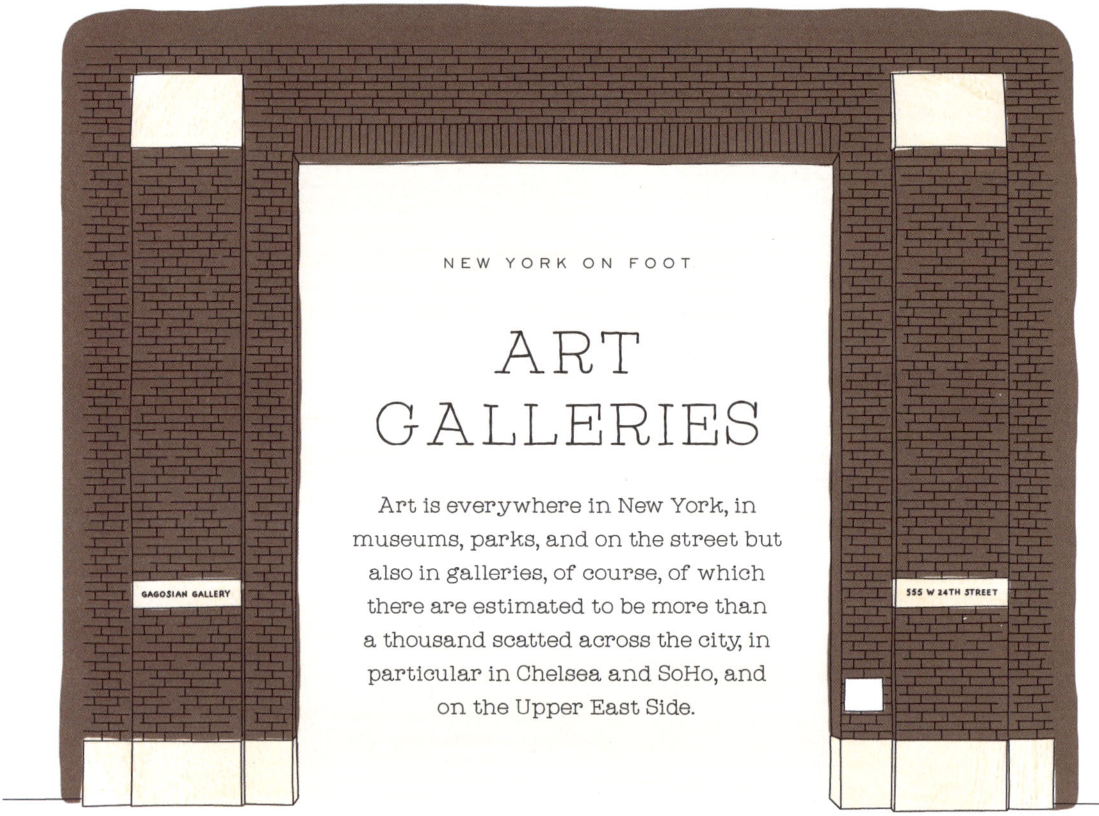

ART GALLERIES

Art is everywhere in New York, in museums, parks, and on the street but also in galleries, of course, of which there are estimated to be more than a thousand scatted across the city, in particular in Chelsea and SoHo, and on the Upper East Side.

The major galleries include the Gagosian in Chelsea, which has shown works by cult artists from Andy Warhol and Jackson Pollock to Miró and Calder, and Acquavella Galleries on the Upper East Side, which boasts names such as Monet, Degas, Picasso, Giacometti, and a host of others.

A number of galleries have begun to open their doors in Brooklyn over the years, in the wake of an exodus of artists who could no longer afford the cost of rent in Manhattan.

Cross the bridge to the Luhring Augustine Gallery's space in Bushwick, featuring large-scale installations and long-term projects with a strong focus on international contemporary art, along with the Moiety Gallery, which also offers studio space for talented young artists.

FLEA MARKETS

Flea markets can be treasure troves or time wasters. Go prepared like a New Yorker. The most interesting items will probably include plates, decorated mugs, furniture, and vintage advertising signboards.

Try to have a fairly clear idea of what you are looking for and bring a trolley for heavier items.

The Chelsea Flea (29 West 25th Street, just around the corner from the Flatiron Building) is open from 8.00 A.M. until 5.00 P.M. every weekend. You can expect to find antiques (some a hundred years old), collector's items, vintage clothes, jewelry, and knickknacks. Admission costs a dollar, a small price to pay to maintain this historic little market, which has been open in this corner of Manhattan since 1976.

The Chelsea Flea joined forced with Hell's Kitchen Flea Market, named by National Geographic as the "best shopping street in the world." Top tip: Don't be afraid to haggle, as it is no secret that prices tend to be inflated for tourists.

The Brooklyn Flea Market held under the Manhattan Bridge boasts around eighty stalls and is open between April and October. A trip here is a great excuse to get out of Manhattan, experience another side of life in the Big Apple, and take a stroll through the newly refurbished neighborhood of Dumbo (Down Under the Manhattan Bridge Overpass).

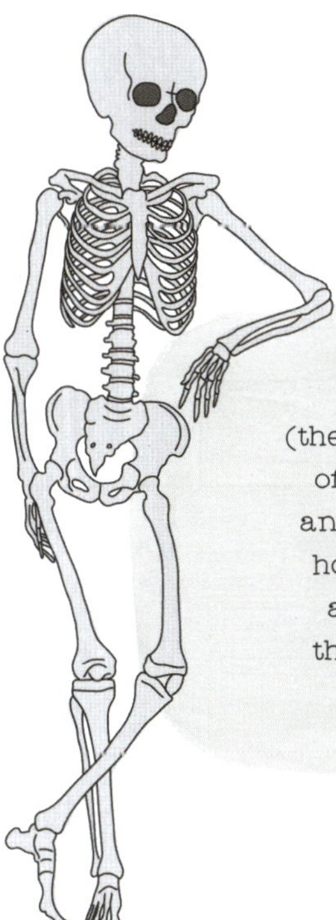

The Oddities Flea Market (theodditiesfleamarket.com) features curios of every kind, from taxidermy animals and anatomical specimens to jewelry and homeware. After taking place each year at Brooklyn Bazaar, in December 2025 the market was held at the Metropolitan Pavilion (125 West 18th Street).

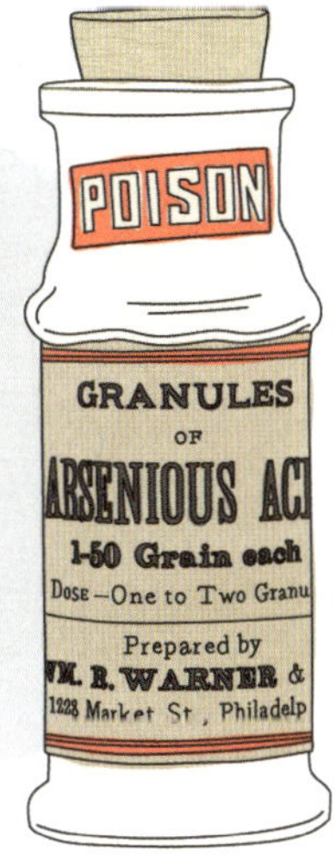

STREET ART

A new kind of art tourism has developed in recent years around street art and murals, and you can now book various guided tours that will take you on foot or by bus to admire and photograph these works, which appear, more or less legally, on the walls of the city. One of the first and most influential artists to create graffiti in New York was Keith Haring in the 1980s, and his work can still be viewed at various locations around the city. His most iconic pieces include *Crack is Wack* in Harlem and the black-and-white murals in the restrooms of the LGBTQ+ Community Center in Greenwich Village.

The Graffiti Hall of Fame, also in Harlem, makes use of the walls of a schoolyard as its canvas. Bear in mind that there is also some graffiti inside the building, so it is wiser to come on a weekday when the place is open.

Street art in Brooklyn

Admirers of street art in Brooklyn should head for the Bushwick neighborhood. The area is in constant flux, with murals popping up everywhere, partly through the efforts of the Bushwick Collective, a nonprofit organization that has drawn artists and projects from around the globe.

SPORTS BARS

You only have to watch Americans enthusiastically cheering on their idols in all kinds of disciplines to see that they are mad about sport. When there's a sporting event on, pretty much any bar in New York can become a sports bar, but some have gained a reputation for their unique atmosphere.

Smithfield Hall in Chelsea is one such venue.

The furnishings are rustic but modern, and with its eleven television screens, this bar styles itself the home of football in New York City. Come and try American contemporary cuisine and a range of seasonal beers.

Standings, in the East Village, is a rather unusual sports bar.

First, because of its size. It is a single room in which, as you might have guessed from the name, it is tricky to find a seat, and secondly because matches are broadcast nonstop but at a very low volume. The walls are plastered with club sports memorabilia, and American football and baseball are the favorite sports.

ROOFTOPS

The moment temperatures permit, locals rush to hotel rooftops to escape the crowds and concrete and enjoy the iconic Manhattan skyline. The unmissable views are from Brooklyn, however, and from the 1 Hotel Brooklyn Bridge in particular, from which there is an amazing panorama.

The Peninsula, a hotel on Fifth Avenue, is another exclusive hideaway where you feel both above the city and still a part of it at the same time. The surroundings might be a little reminiscent of old New York, but the cocktail list is absolutely cutting edge.

OVERSTORY

Overstory

This elegant cocktail bar offers cocktails complete with a stunning view over the heart of the Financial District. Located on the 64th floor of 70 Pine Street, it boasts a spectacular, circular observation deck with 360-degree views across the New York skyline. Enjoy a warm and sophisticated welcome in this venue where the meticulous mixology and incredible views from the terrace have made it one of the most celebrated bars in the city.

Jimmy rooftop bar

There are spectacular views from JIMMY, the rooftop bar of the ModernHaus hotel in the heart of SoHo, which boasts large picture windows looking out over the city and even an outdoor area with a swimming pool. It's the perfect place for an after-dinner cocktail, even in winter.

COMEDY CLUBS

THE Broadway COMEDY CLUB

New Yorkers have a reputation for being a bit surly, but this is largely because their sense of humor tends to be sarcastic and self-deprecating. A good way to get a feel for this is to see a stand-up comedy show.

Comics are very likely to do audience work during shows, especially if they detect an accent of some kind, so it is important to be prepared and laugh along with everybody else.

The most famous clubs include the Broadway Comedy Club in Hell's Kitchen, which played host to comedy giants like Robin Williams and Andy Kaufman back in the day. The Comedy Cellar, in the heart of Greenwich Village, has hosted Amy Schumer, Kevin Hart, and Aziz Ansari (comedycellar.com), while you might bump into Tracy Morgan or Louis C.K. at the EastVille Comedy Club, in Brooklyn.

DANCING

Dance lovers, you have set foot in the right place.

If you are still suffering from jet lag and waking up early in the morning, or if you just don't want to stay up too late, one alternative is a Party Brunch (or Bottomless Brunch), which, as the name suggests, is a brunch organized like an evening party, with blaring music and bottles of champagne ordered to your table.

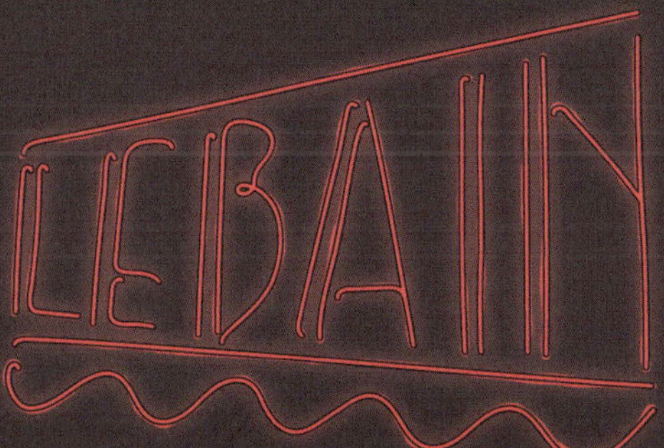

Manhattan and clubs

The Standard Hotel in the Meatpacking District deserves a mention. Under one roof, you will find a restaurant, beer garden, and rooftop bar in which to enjoy a sundowner, and a club laid out over two floors (one indoors, one outdoors) that even boasts a jacuzzi for the more adventurous.

Alternative nights

Other discos of note include LAVO, where superstar DJs like Christopher Lawrence and Tiësto have spun the decks; the House of Yes in Brooklyn, known for its more alternative celebrations in conjunction with Burning Man, the famous (but crazy) festival held in the Nevada desert every year; Bembe in Williamsburg, which plays casual Afrobeat; and The Box in Nolita, which is burlesque-themed.

COOL BOOKSTORES

Bauman Rare Books (485 Madison Avenue)

This absolutely beautiful bookstore, with its Persian carpets and wood paneling, has a constantly changing inventory of over four thousand books. The ideal spot for serious collectors and browsers looking for an original gift idea.

Community Bookstore (143 Seventh Avenue, Park Slope, Brooklyn)

Not to be missed by fans of niche bookstores, this outlet has been open since 1971 and is renowned for stocking the coolest titles, for its children's reading circles, and for the cat that wanders among the shelves. There's even a piano that some customers stop by to play.

Rizzoli Bookstore (1133 Broadway and 26th Street)

This store has been an institution for more than fifty years, both for those seeking books in Italian and anyone with an interest in beautiful things. The bookstore was founded by the brilliant publisher Angelo Rizzoli in 1964 and stocks a wide variety of illustrated photo books on art, architecture, and other subjects. Its rooms are so beautiful that the store has been used as a movie location on several occasions; remember *Falling in Love* (1984)?

Powerhouse Books Arena (28 Adams Street, Dumbo, Brooklyn)

This is not just a bookstore but a laboratory for creative minds in whose small amphitheater readings and literary debates are held, in addition to all kinds of events and performances at which you may find yourself rubbing shoulders with Pulitzer Prize winners and political commentators.

GOSPEL

Originating in African-American church congregations, gospel is a Christian music genre that mainly consists of hymns accompanied by hand-clapping. The best, and most authentic, way to experience this art form is to go to any church in Harlem and attend a service.

Remember that these are places of worship, so arrive a bit early to get settled in a pew. It's bad form to leave before the end of the service, and you should dress and behave appropriately, of course.

Holiness unto the Lord

Some of the churches renowned for their gospel choirs and the warm welcome extended to tourists are Bethel Gospel Assembly (on 120th Street) and Canaan Baptist Church of Christ (on 116th Street). If you want to go to a gospel service without leaving Manhattan, head for Times Square Church (on 51st Street), whose premises are an old theater building.

PROHIBITION

Prohibition was a period during which neither the sale nor the consumption of alcohol was permitted, and it began in the United States in 1919. The intention had been to reduce the criminality associated with the trafficking of drink, but it had precisely the opposite effect, especially in New York City, where it was never possible to put the ban into practice. Indeed, thanks to the famous speakeasies, corruption and crime were to flourish during those years.

THE AMERICAN ISSUE

WESTERVILLE, OHIO, JANUARY 25, 1919

U.S. IS VOTED DRY

36th STATE RATIFIES DRY AMENDMENT JAN. 16

Speakeasies

Speakeasies were clandestine drinking holes accessed via the most unlikely entrances, usually in an adjacent establishment. The name itself conveys the secret nature of such venues, in and about which you would "speak softly" to avoid attracting the attention of the police. Only a handful of the original speakeasies remain in business, but new ones have opened where you can still get a taste of the transgressive and slightly *film noir*-ish feel of the past. The Prohibition era was definitively considered to have come to an end by late 1933.

The Back Room

The most (in)famous speakeasy is The Back Room in Norfolk Street on the Lower East Side, which has preserved its original decor from the 1920s, a time when gangsters like Lucky Luciano would sit at its small tables.

Entrance to Please Don't Tell, on St Marks Place in the East Village, is via a phone booth, and guided tours are also available for those with an interest in this period of history.

NEW YORK ON SCREEN

We can all watch movies about New York and dream of an idyllic life in the city, but the people who actually live there may have to suppress a wry smile at how reality is presented: penniless young people living in apartments entirely beyond the means of most twenty-somethings, who in the course of a single phone call are miraculously transported from Uptown to the Financial District in a matter of minutes. All beautiful illusions, but real life is clearly very different.

The Soup Nazi

A memorable scene for many New Yorkers is from the *Seinfeld* episode entitled "The Soup Nazi," in which the two main characters go to a really popular place to order soup known as the best you can get anywhere in the city—served by the most horrible person in the world. The outlet eventually became a chain called The Original Soupman (long since closed, but now reopened as The Original Soup Kitchen).

You can spot where various movies or sitcoms were filmed pretty much anywhere in New York, and there are countless themed tours.

On the Upper East Side alone, you can see The Pierre, the hotel where Chandler and Monica get married in *Friends*, the Tiffany megastore, after which the unforgettable movie with Audrey Hepburn is named; the St. Regis Hotel where some of *The Devil Wears Prada* (2006) is set; and the equally luxurious Waldorf-Astoria from *Coming to America* (1998).

LITERARY NEW YORK

New York has always attracted writers as a destination, not just because so many found fame in the Big Apple but also due to the number and concentration of publishing houses in the city. The old stereotype of the penniless artist living in a garret in Brooklyn has changed over the years. Plenty of famous artists live in Brooklyn these days, although they can't be short of money any more, given how house prices have skyrocketed, including the likes of the late Paul Auster, Jennifer Egan, Jonathan Safran Foer, and many others, with whom you may end up rubbing shoulders in local bakeries and cafés.

POETS CAFE

Up-and-coming writers often perform at bars and clubs, which organize open-mic evenings where anyone can get up on stage and recite poetry or read extracts from novels. The best-known include The Moth StorySLAM (75 Broad Street) and the Nuyorican Poets Cafe (236 East 3rd Street), which the Beat writer Allen Ginsberg called "the most integrated place on the planet."

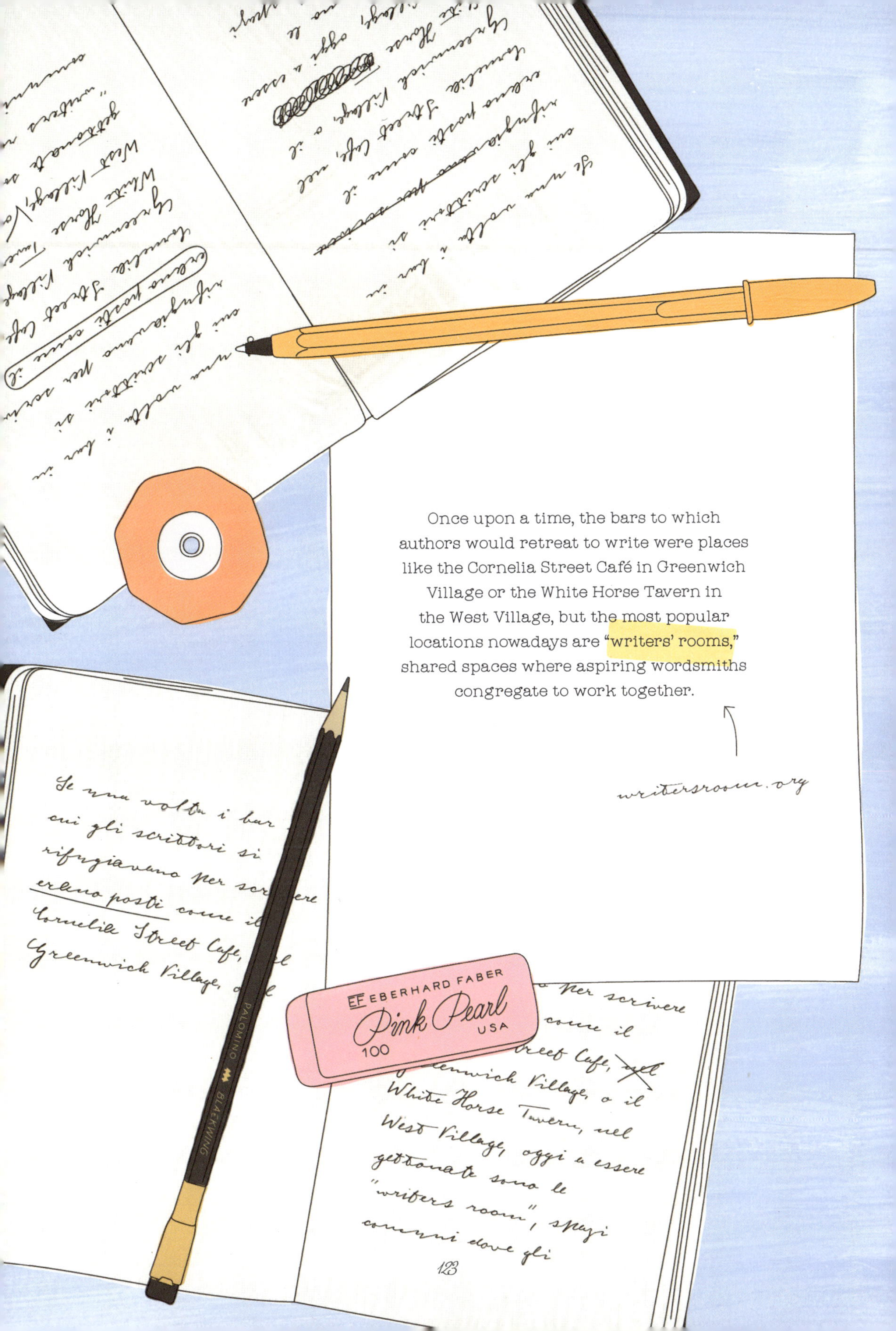

Once upon a time, the bars to which authors would retreat to write were places like the Cornelia Street Café in Greenwich Village or the White Horse Tavern in the West Village, but the most popular locations nowadays are "writers' rooms," shared spaces where aspiring wordsmiths congregate to work together.

writersroom.org

INSTAGRAM CITY

If you want to stand out from the hordes of tourists taking selfies in front of the Statue of Liberty, take your cue from the locals and point your lens at the streets. Capture the essence of the city with a photo of New York city and its signature yellow cabs at sunset, or maybe a portrait of the Flower District, a small, green oasis in the heart of Manhattan located on West 28th Street between Sixth and Seventh Avenues, which would definitely be a more original subject.

New Yorkers are obsessed with posting pictures of food.

Maybe it's just fashionable, maybe it's because the food in NYC is particularly memorable, but the hashtag #nyceats is trending, so be smart in finding colorful, quirky dishes and your Instagram feed will blow up in no time! Some especially photogenic locations include Pietro in Nolita (a bar that is entirely pink), Roberta's pizzeria in Brooklyn (good, hipster food), and DŌ cookie dough at 16 Handles (various locations; check opening times first).

Get an unusual angle on the city for your photos. From the top floors of the Deutsche Bank Center (formerly the Time Warner Center) on Columbus Circle, for example, from which you have a perfect view of Central Park and a chance to capture some extraordinary images.

TALES OF THE CITY

It has been said over and over again that once you've lived in New York, it's impossible to live anywhere else, but why is this the case?

New Yorkers are unable to kick certain vices to which they have become accustomed, such as not needing to own a car to get around, thanks to the convenience of a public transit network that is genuinely comprehensive.

But that is by no means all the city has to offer. Other reasons include better career opportunities then elsewhere; the sheer number of delis and bodegas, which make going shopping a mere stroll down the steps in front of your own home; the instant access to any item or service you could possibly need 24/7; and the size of the city, which, despite being a metropolis, manages to feel like a village in parts of some neighborhoods.

"Once you have lived in New York and it has become your home, no place else is good enough. All of everything is concentrated here ... It is all of everything. It goes all right. It is tireless and its air is charged with energy."

(John Steinbeck)

TALES OF THE CITY *(the downsides)*

One of the phenomena about which many New Yorkers complain is gentrification.

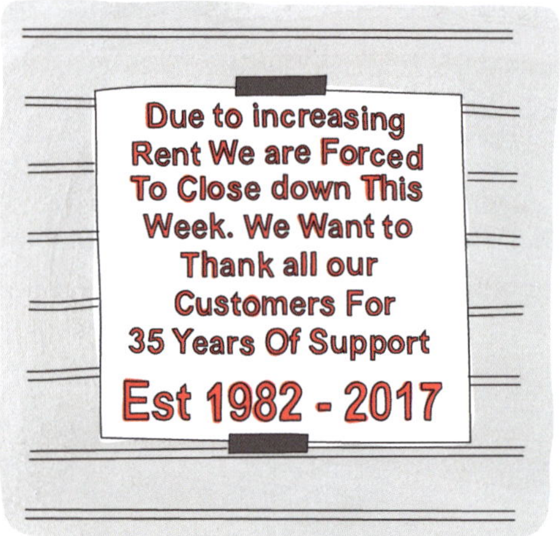

What does the term mean? Gentrification is the process whereby neighborhoods once imbued with the culture of its residents, who are often immigrants, are culturally impoverished as the areas become increasingly hip and the rents high. Prohibitive costs mean that independent stores or small brands are harder to find, and, as a rule, local firms are becoming scarcer. The only growing businesses are large multinational corporations that can afford imposing offices and branches.

"*New York is an ugly city, a dirty city. Its climate is a scandal, its politics are used to frighten children, its traffic is madness, its competition is murderous. But there is one thing about it—once you have lived in New York and it has become your home, no place else is good enough.*"

(John Steinbeck)

NEW YORK FOR FREE

New York may be one of the world's most expensive cities, but there are lots of things you can do for free.

Don't underestimate the potential of municipal parks. New Yorkers' weekend activities include going for a jog, getting food from a food truck, and having an impromptu picnic.

In winter, you can enjoy skating on the ice rinks, although the only free one is in Bryant Park. You can make up what you spend at the Winter Village market with what you save on skating!

THE PUBLIC.

Lots of public parks screen movies or stage plays during the summer, Shakespeare in the Park being the most famous. The players of The Public Theater troupe perform one of the Bard's works at the Delacorte Theater in Central Park every year.

The New York Public Library, the High Line, and the museum at the Fashion Institute of Technology also charge no admission.

NEW YORK WITH CHILDREN

One of the best places for children to let off a little steam in safety is Chelsea Piers, a complex with a wide range of drop-in facilities that don't require booking in advance.

CHELSEA PIERS
NEW YORK
EST. NY 1995

The various activities on offer include yoga, music, sports (such as basketball and soccer), and even cooking classes, in which you can learn how to make healthy and nutritious snacks.

Children's Museum of the Arts

Many museums are suitable for children, and some are even intended specifically for them, including the Children's Museum of the Arts in Greenwich Village, which boasts a "clay bar" where the kids can create all kinds of fantastic creatures with their own hands, under the guidance of the staff.

Other entertaining places include Taiyaki in Lower Manhattan, where they serve ice cream in fun, fish-shaped cones; Alice's Tea Cup (102 W 73rd Street), where everything, even brunch, is Alice-in-Wonderland-themed; and Van Leeuwen (stores across Manhattan).

NEW YORK CONFIDENTIAL

The Whispering Gallery is located on the lower-level dining area of Grand Central Station, in the gallery next to the Oyster Bar. The extraordinary thing about these arches is that if you stand in one corner and whisper something, a person standing on the opposite corner will be able to hear you perfectly.

It's a great little trick for surprising your traveling companions.

The many and varied attractions of the Rockefeller Center are an open secret, but less well known is the beautiful garden on the rooftop that is open to visitors and commands stunning views over the city.

A small cut-through for pedestrians runs all the way from 51st Street to 57th Street between Sixth and Seventh Avenues in the middle of Midtown. It is known as 6½ Avenue and is the only thoroughfare of its kind in the city. The whole thing is about a quarter of a mile (400 m) long and a stroll along it makes a speedy shortcut to the charming fountain in Paley Park.

When the city has tired you out, it is the perfect spot to find a bit of peace and quiet.

New York's street art has transformed the East Village and the Lower East Side into an open-air gallery. Freeman Alley offers a narrow tunnel filled with ever-changing graffiti, stickers, and stencils, while First Street Green Art Park features a rotation of murals and cultural events. Hidden artworks appear across facades and shutters of the local area. The Houston Bowery Mural has become a canvas for international artists, while St Marks Place and the surrounding streets are a whirl of colors, dark alleys, and street art. Together, these neighborhoods showcase the urban creativity to be found in Manhattan. The city even boasts five sections of the Berlin Wall.

New York never ceases to amaze. Keep your eyes open.

NEW YORK AND MUSIC

New Yorkers love listening to live music. The genre on offer will depend on the neighborhood you find yourself in. You will hear hip-hop in Brooklyn, for example, Times Square is famous for commercial music, and they listen to electronic/pop on the Lower East Side. While the Bronx is known for reggaeton, the Upper East Side is renowned for its jazz, which can also be heard in Harlem and Greenwich Village.

City dwellers get to hear music almost everywhere, and buskers are often playing on the streets, in Central Park, or in subway tunnels.

New Yorkers are usually big fans of such musicians, except when they perform in subway cars, where they have broken one of the city's fundamental rules: avoid eye contact with strangers on the train.

MERCURY LOUNGE

Some of the most popular places with locals include the Mercury Lounge (217 E Houston Street, on the Lower East Side), which mainly features alternative rock.

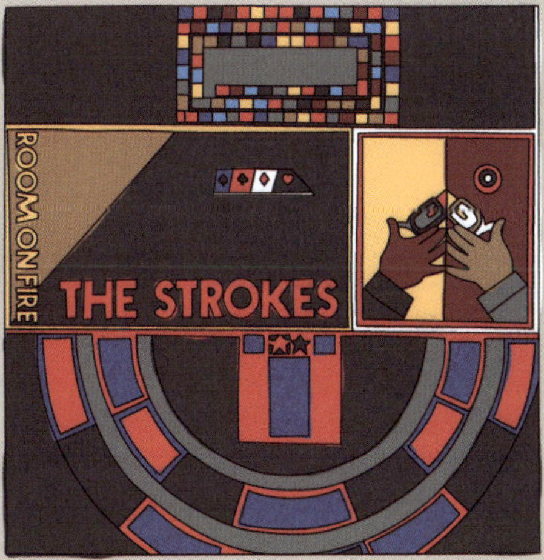

It was not by chance that this was the place that started the careers of bands like The Strokes. Musicians such as Jeff Buckley, Lou Reed, and The Killers have also played here.

FIDI

You are most likely to run into tourists and white-collar workers from banks and financial institutions in the Financial District, so the neighborhood is full of fancy restaurants and cool spots to while away happy hour.

Nobu Matsuhisa, the star Japanese chef, has also decided to open a place in FiDi, and Nobu Downtown at 195 Broadway is an elegant restaurant with a bar above it where you can sample sophisticated cocktails before descending to the dining room on the floor below. Guaranteed to be overrun by locals.

If you happen to find yourself in FiDi during the day, but want to avoid the more touristy parts, one option might be the Elevated Acre at 55 Water Street, a rooftop park with a beautiful view that has become popular with workers during their lunchbreak.

MANHATTAN BY NEIGHBORHOOD
CHINATOWN
Joe's Ginger
錦江飯店
健康堂
Health Trail Co
Cindy Hair Salon
Joe's Ginger 錦江飯店
喜運来大酒家
佛有緣
VEGETARIAN DIM SUM HOUSE
素
VEGETARIA
DELIGHT 28 RESTAURANT INC
AHEAD
STOP
SCHOOL

Chinatown is mostly inhabited by Asian Americans and is very popular with tourists. New Yorkers flock here for the delicious food enjoyed by so many (dim sum, boiled or fried dumplings, and so on).

Another attraction that draws locals to this bustling neighborhood is the shopping. Chinatown is the place to find everything, from the usual souvenirs to bits of hi-tech, medicines, traditional Chinese herbs, and foot reflexology clinics.

Essentially, there's something for everyone.

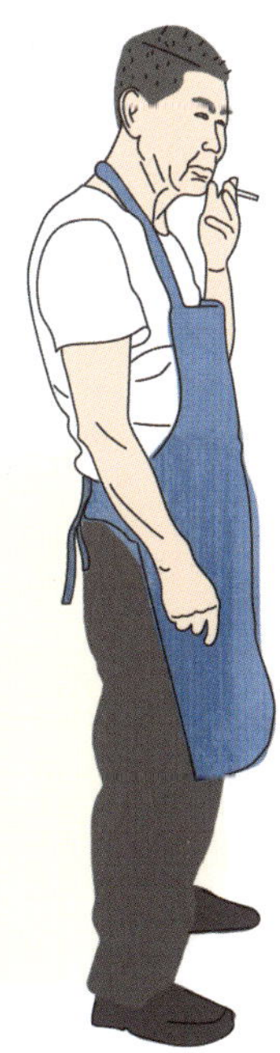

Chinatown also boasts one of the bloodiest streets in New York, if not the whole of America: Doyers Street, nicknamed "the Bloody Angle," was the scene of numerous killings among the Tong gangs of the early twentieth century. **Did you know?** Axes were often the weapon of choice for gangsters.

LITTLE ITALY

The once thriving neighborhood of Little Italy has now been swallowed up by the surrounding districts of Chinatown, NoHo, and Nolita. With visitor numbers falling, it is now little more than a single thoroughfare (Mulberry Street), and Italian food or typical Italian products are now available pretty much everywhere.

Another Little Italy is on the rise, however, this time around Arthur Avenue in the Bronx, where Lady Gaga shot the video for "Eh, Eh (Nothing Else I Can Say)." The restaurants, stores, and products available here have remained traditional, however, which is probably more to do with the lower footfall compared with busier Manhattan.

Little Italy is restored to its past glories during the Feast of San Gennaro, held over a few days in mid-September, when Mulberry Street and the surrounding streets are flooded with exquisite Italian food and a famous eating competition is held to see who can force down the most cannoli.
S.GENNARO

MANHATTAN BY NEIGHBORHOOD
TRIBECA

Tribeca (Triangle Below Canal Street) was the place to be for artists and rock stars, during the 1970s in particular.

House prices have skyrocketed over the years and creative types have made way for actors and celebrities, turning the area these days into a fashionable residential neighborhood.

TRIBECA FILM FESTIVAL

Tribeca is still worth a visit for its art galleries and museums, but the event that draws in thousands of New Yorkers every year is the Tribeca Film Festival held between April and May, during which you can catch previews of independent movies and attend panel discussions about cinema, and even run into a celebrity or two.

GREAT STORIES ARE TIMELESS

SOHO

Much like Tribeca, SoHo was once a neighborhood of artists, but it has now become extremely expensive and is often used as a pied-à-terre by wealthy families. The people who choose to live here are drawn by both the area's post-industrial feel and the vibrancy of its bars and restaurants.

BALTHAZAR
RESTAURANT

Balthazar at 80 Spring Street is a historic bistro with a great reputation for the best French cuisine, and the onion soup and the hamburgers come particularly highly recommended. If you wish to eat here, you will need to be patient and wait in line, or book well in advance.

Prince Street, Greene Street, and Wooster Street are just a few of the main shopping streets in SoHo. It's easy to find the big brands in these areas, but it is better to buy from independent stores to avoid paying import duty and ending up in the same clothes as everyone else.

Fun fact: The acronym SoHo (South of Houston Street) has nothing to do with the eponymous area in London, whose name apparently comes from a hunting cry dating back to the seventeenth century.

CHELSEA

The cityscape here is quite different from the rest of the island. In some parts, the predominantly brownstone buildings lend the neighborhood a chic and vaguely European feel.

Elsewhere, however, there is a preponderance of new and super-luxurious residential buildings that remind visitors they are in upmarket Manhattan.

The famous High Line and Chelsea Market are in Chelsea, as is the Meatpacking District, one of the areas that is most popular with locals for its shopping, and for its nightlife in particular, with places like Catch (21 Ninth Avenue), Gansevoort Meatpacking (18 Ninth Avenue), Somewhere Nowhere (112 West 25th Street), The Standard High Line Hotel (848 Washington Street), and Petite (161 West 23rd Street).

HUDSON YARDS

NEW YORK

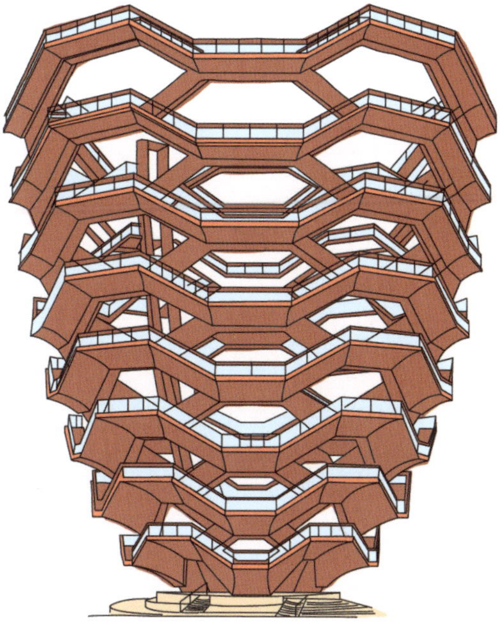

Of the residential complexes that have changed the face of the neighborhood, Hudson Yards is worthy of particular note, extending some 28 acres (11 hectares) across what was once a train depot near the northern end of the High Line. At its center is the Vessel, an imposing and whimsical metal monument, sixteen stories tall, created by Thomas Heatherwick. Its strange beehive of 154 flights of steps is slightly reminiscent of the impossible architecture of M. C. Escher.

This art installation has already been nicknamed the "Eiffel Tower of the Big Apple" and is one of the area's main attractions.

The Shed, the first New York cultural center conceived to produce and host every kind of art discipline, from the performing arts to visual art and pop culture, opened its doors in Hudson Yards in the spring of 2019. The building is made up of a telescoping outer shell, a space called The McCourt, which can accommodate an audience of 2,220, a theater, and two exhibition spaces.

LOWER EAST SIDE & THE EAST VILLAGE

This was once the place for grunge, the haunt of aspiring musicians and people living on the so-called fringes of society, but it has now become a bastion of downtown chic. It is known for its leather district and is famous for its bars and restaurants.

Visitors to the Lower East Side looking for entertainment that is somewhere between chic and underground will find it at Miss Lily's (109 Avenue A), a Caribbean oasis with food, music, and superb rum-based cocktails that guarantee you a fun time.

The East Village was New York's punk neighborhood and, although it has undergone significant change since the 1970s, it is still mainly inhabited by young people. Take a stroll down its streets and you will notice a more relaxed vibe than in many other areas, with small stores selling inexpensive and original knickknacks, plenty of tattoo parlors, and gig venues.

GREENWICH VILLAGE

The first thing to be aware of when talking about the Village is that New Yorkers pronounce it "Gren-itch," so saying it correctly is a good place to start. The neighborhood is known for its activism, and for the gay rights movement in the 1970s in particular, and it has gained a reputation as a bohemian spot, although now it is mainly residential and the sort of place where families live and the baker knows his customers by name.

The area has slowly lost its blighted reputation in part due to one of its most illustrious fictional residents, Carrie Bradshaw.

The apartment of the famous fashionista and writer from the cult TV series *Sex and the City* was indeed set in this very district, although the real aspiration of most New Yorkers is not to have a closet like Carrie's but to find a rent-controlled apartment like hers.

Bleecker Street is the place to come to properly experience the Village, as it is affectionately known to locals. This fascinating thoroughfare is lined with big-brand stores and small local boutiques such as the Mûre + Grand (at 319 Bleecker Street), which has fantastic leather goods. Chloe's (at 185), a vegan restaurant beloved of celebrities, is recommended as a place to eat.

Good to know: Greenwich has the same pronunciation as the London district through which the famous prime meridian passes.

MIDTOWN

This area is mainly populated by workers and tourists, so New Yorkers without a real reason to come here tend to avoid it as much as they can. The concentration of corporate employees and out-of-towners makes it one of the busiest neighborhoods in Manhattan for noise, people, and light pollution.

The disproportionate number of offices in the area explains the higher concentration of places for lunch than elsewhere in the city, some of which are quite reasonably priced. Keep an eye out for the many rather charming small parks and gardens where workers can enjoy a sandwich in peace.

There are some residential areas with lower footfall in Midtown, especially near the United Nations Headquarters in the Turtle Bay neighborhood, a collection of streets leading down to the East River. Look out for the apartment complex called Tudor City, located at the far end of 40th Street, which dates back to 1927 and is thought to be the first residential skyscraper to be built anywhere in the world.

Within the main lobby of the United Nations Headquarters on First Avenue, between 42nd and 48th Streets, you will find a meditation room that is open to all visitors. It offers an ideal way to visit this famous building and perhaps soak up a little of the energy of those striving to change the world day in, day out.

UPPER WEST SIDE

The residents of this area are mostly families, so it is lively during the day, with plenty of activity and stores of every kind, but things tend to be very quiet in the evenings. Apart from the occasional bar and restaurant, the nightlife is not especially exciting.

Big Apple inhabitants consider this one of the more accessible neighborhoods, although it is still cool. Plenty of celebrities live here, especially in the area adjoining Central Park West.

THE SHOPS AT COLUMBUS CIRCLE

Local shopping spots of choice include Bloomingdale's Outlet Store (2085 Broadway), the perfect place for people who like labels but don't wish to spend a fortune, and the Deutsche Bank Center at 10 Columbus Circle, which is a towering complex housing Whole Foods, a very popular grocery store with New Yorkers who are increasingly interested in all things organic, along with a host of stores, bars, restaurants, and a space dedicated to live music (Jazz at Lincoln Center).

jazz

Jacob's Pickles fills up on weekends with New Yorkers heading to brunch.

The Upper West Side is extremely popular with people seeking a bit of peace and quiet after the chaos of Midtown, and such refuges include Jacob's Pickles at 680 Columbus Avenue, between 93rd and 94th Streets ...

... and Barney Greengrass at 541 Amsterdam Avenue, a historic Jewish delicatessen that opened its doors nearly 120 years ago. It has acquired a reputation for smoked fish, and you must try not just the wild salmon, but also the smoked sturgeon, dill-cured gravlax, and the exquisitely delicate sable. Do note that you can only pay cash here.

UPPER EAST SIDE

There was a time when the Upper East Side was the haunt of such figures as Frank Sinatra and, a little later, Woody Allen, whose regular Wednesday evening appearances at the Carlyle on 76th Street were long the worst-kept secret in Manhattan. Such times are now but a memory, however.

Most people now consider the neighborhood rather snobbish and dull, although it remains the chicest, whether you like it or not. A short stroll along Madison Avenue between 57th and 70th Streets is enough to confirm this.

Locals like to treat themselves to elegant lunches in The Mark Hotel (25 East 77th Street).

Sant Ambroeus & Casa Lever

Two more places of interest for foodies: Sant Ambroeus at 1000 Madison Avenue was opened in 1982 by the same family who had founded the elegant tea room of the same name on Corso Matteotti in Milan in 1936 (they have two other branches in New York and one in Southampton in New York State). Casa Lever at 390 Park Avenue, also founded by Italians, has become a rendezvous for the world's leading businessmen, with cuisine to match.

The Upper East Side often hosts art exhibitions and fashion shows.

The Park Avenue Armory up by 67th Street is an iconic spot. This historic complex was built as a headquarters for the 7th New York Militia Regiment in 1870 and the building, part palace, part industrial warehouse, was one of the attractions that led New Yorkers to re-evaluate their opinions of the whole area.

YORKVILLE

The Upper East Side is basically divided into two parts: the extremely chic and exorbitantly expensive area around Park Avenue, and Yorkville, where prices are a little more affordable. Historically the area has been home to Hungarians and Germans, and even today is mostly occupied by native New Yorkers and Europeans.

If it's been cheaper to live here than elsewhere in Manhattan, that has been because of its distance from subway stations, although the opening of a stop on the Q line has rapidly changed this.

Carl Schurz Park

Carl Schurz Park, a green space of around 15 acres (6 hectares), looking out over the East River, is very popular with locals and would be an ideal place to take a stroll or sit on a bench and watch the yachts rolling in from Long Island.

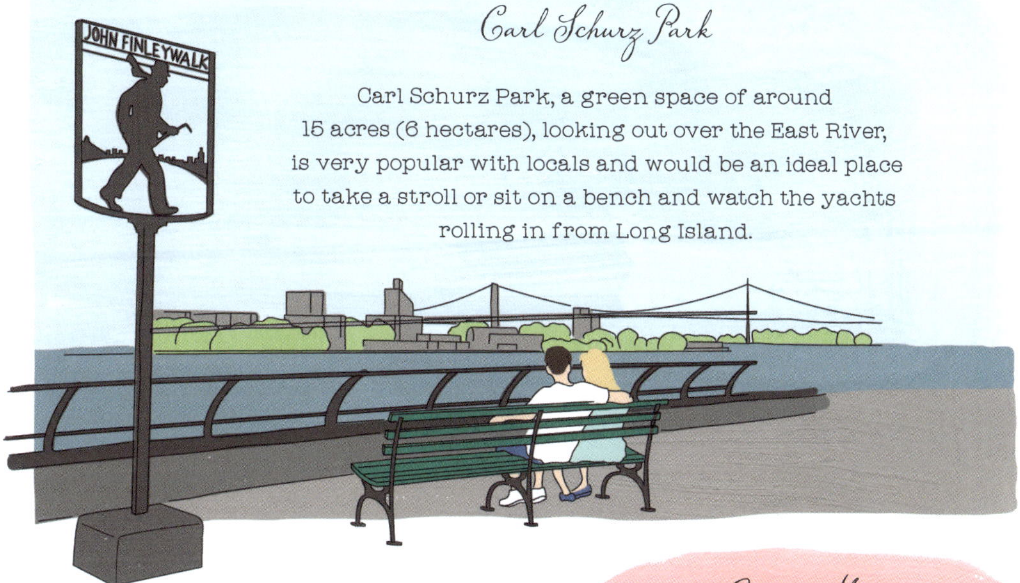

Gracie Mansion

Gracie Mansion, the official residence of New York City's mayor, was built in the Federal style in 1799. The hill behind the house is popular with locals for its beautiful view across the river.

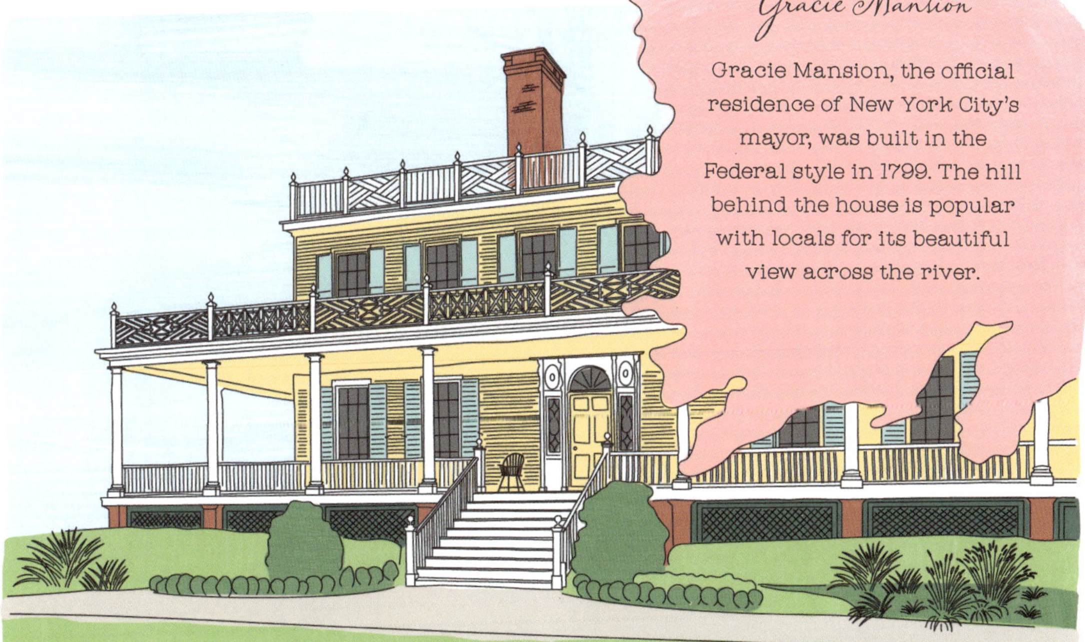

With their wooden floors and high ceilings, the buildings in Yorkville are described as pre-war, as they were constructed in the early twentieth century. The area is full of small restaurants and mom-and-pop stores to explore.

HARLEM

Harlem is historically associated with Black culture, but less well known is that, for a time, it was the real Little Italy of Manhattan and the place with the highest concentration of Italians in the United States; traces of this past are still visible.

One such example is Rao's restaurant (455 East 114th Street) with its signature bright red entrance livery, which opened its doors in 1896. Don't forget to book well in advance.

Harlem was considered a fairly dangerous neighborhood in the past, but the situation has changed radically, and the population is increasingly made up of people who are changing the face of the whole area and boosting house prices.

The Red Rooster (310 Malcolm X Blvd) is undoubtedly the place to be, as the restaurant serves all the comfort food you would expect to find in the southern United States: fried chicken, cornbread, meatballs, and other treats.

BROOKLYN

DUMBO

Dumbo (Down Under the Manhattan Bridge Overpass) is the city's latest star area, with a fantastic view of Manhattan but without its traffic, and a host of new bars, chic restaurants, French bakeries, and stores with fashionable wares at prices that are still affordable, at least for the moment. Dumbo has also been chosen as the location for SoHo House's Brooklyn branch, known, naturally enough, as DUMBO House.

JANE'S CAROUSEL
BROOKLYN BRIDGE PARK

Tourists and locals flock to Jane's Carousel in Brooklyn Bridge Park, a beautiful and authentic carousel dating back to 1922, although the glazed square shelter was designed by Ateliers Jean Nouvel in 2011.

The location is often used for photoshoots, and you are very likely to see couples in formal wear, strolling along the waterfront on their way back from their wedding.

Locals to this part of Brooklyn can even choose to dip a toe in the East River at Pebble Beach (weather permitting). The water is actually quite clean in this part of the river, to the extent that there is even an organization called the Brooklyn Bridge Park Boathouse who will take you on a free 20-minute kayak tour in the summer, an unusual experience that is not well publicized, so take advantage of it.

BROOKLYN BRIDGE PARK BOATHOUSE

BROOKLYN HEIGHTS

Manhattan seems conceptually a world away from the tranquil residential areas and signature brownstone (in fact, red sandstone) town houses here. Brooklyn Heights offers a great opportunity for locals to get away from the chaos and enjoy a little peace and quiet.

Brooklyn Heights once attracted artists and writers like W.H. Auden, Salvador Dalí, and Truman Capote. Its proximity to the Financial District, however, has since drawn more residents working in banking and insurance.

Make sure to take a stroll on the Promenade, a pedestrian and cycle path looking out over the East River with beautiful views of the Financial District and the rest of Lower Manhattan. Sometimes it's nice to give the Big Apple some love from a safe distance!

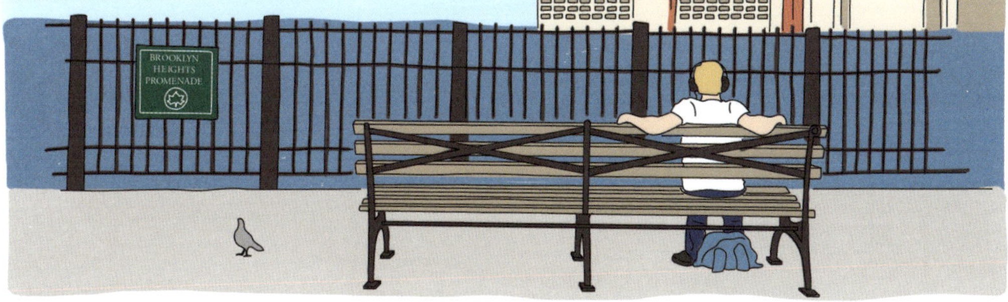

One very chic street is Montague Street, a riot of indie stores and small restaurants much beloved of Brooklyn Heights locals, as witnessed in Bob Dylan's famous song "Tangled Up In Blue."

WILLIAMSBURG

This was the first neighborhood that opened the floodgates for Brooklyn.

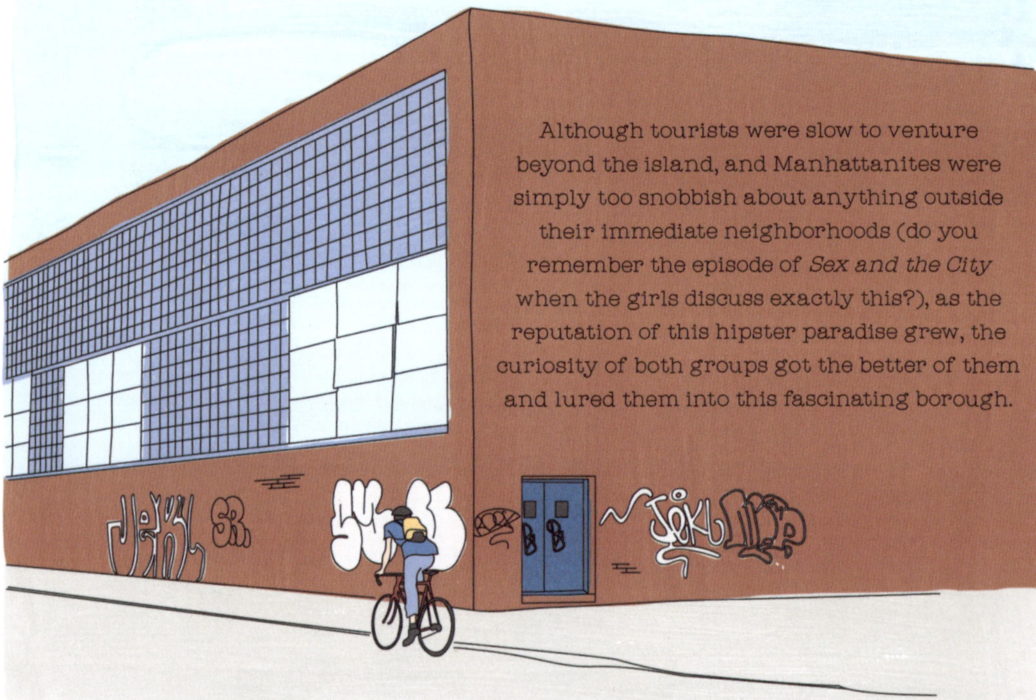

Although tourists were slow to venture beyond the island, and Manhattanites were simply too snobbish about anything outside their immediate neighborhoods (do you remember the episode of *Sex and the City* when the girls discuss exactly this?), as the reputation of this hipster paradise grew, the curiosity of both groups got the better of them and lured them into this fascinating borough.

The hipsters—young, alternative, bohemian, and mainly middle-class locals—are extremely proud of "their" Brooklyn Brewery, the neighborhood beerhouse in operation since 1988 and now also open for guided tours. As you may know, if you meet a hipster, a craft beer is never far away ... (only joking).

DEVOCIÓN

WILLIAMSBURG

Visit Grand Street to soak up the atmosphere of a neighborhood crammed with vintage stores, salons specializing in nail art, and a host of excellent cafés, including Devoción (148 Grand Street).

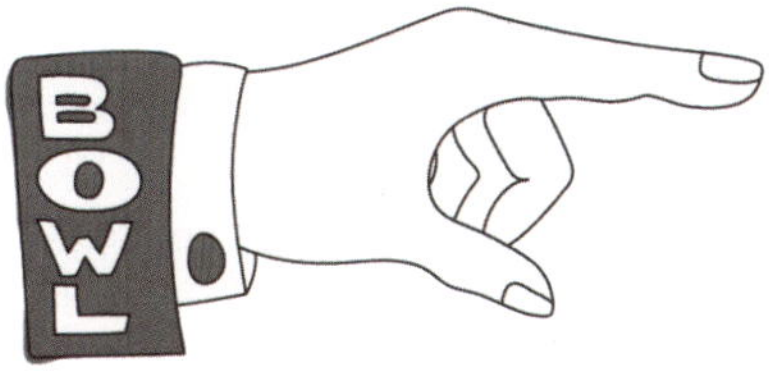

The Brooklyn Bowl at 61 Wythe Avenue is a bar that is half bowling alley, half music venue. It stages gigs and is popular with locals.

There are more than just hipsters in Williamsburg, however. A large part of the neighborhood is home to one of New York's largest communities of Orthodox Jews, and a stroll through the streets of this neighborhood is like stepping back in time, with most locals in traditional clothing and many signs written in Yiddish.

BUSHWICK

Bushwick has transformed from an industrial area to a neighborhood of hipsters and artists in almost no time. An army of creatives has moved in here, taking advantage of the large, abandoned factory buildings and transforming the spaces into lofts and artists' studios as the streets turn into open-air art galleries.

The streets to check out if you have an interest in murals are Jefferson Street and Wyckoff Avenue.

Bushwick has now lost its reputation as one of Brooklyn's most dangerous areas, thanks to this new "artistic" population. Criminality is reducing and the entire area has a strong community feel of mutual support, as witnessed by the numerous bookstores and art galleries.

You can rub shoulders with local emerging artists at work over coffee at Headrest Coffee (262 Irving Avenue) or at The Bushwick Starr (207 Starr Street), a theater with a great range of good beers and excellent cocktails that stages a succession of innovative and avant-garde shows.

It's not unusual for Manhattan residents to ditch their own island in favor of sampling a pizza at Roberta's (261 Moore Street), rated as one of the best in the whole city.

For themed brunch, try Queen Bar & Restaurant (247 Starr Street), which serves Mediterranean food; the Dromedary Urban Tiki Bar (266 Irving Avenue), with its striking industrial decor; or Gordo's Cantina (140 St Nicholas Avenue), for a Mexican twist. Bushwick also hosts secret raves in in unobtrusive, abandoned factory spaces—difficult to track down since the locations are in constant flux.

THE BRONX

The Bronx is most famous for an ignominious past of gangs, drug-dealing, and murder. A process of decriminalization began in the 1980s, since when the population has grown and the neighborhood has become a lot safer. You should stay on your guard, however.

This transformation has continued in recent years and the Bronx has become one of the boroughs with an increasing reputation for its excellent food. A number of chefs who found fame elsewhere in the city have chosen to return to their beloved Bronx to open a restaurant—Ghetto Gastro is just one example. This chefs' collective is making a name for itself through the group's catering operations and their ambition to create dishes and events that will help rehabilitate the neighborhood. Their pop-up dinners have gone viral on Instagram.

New Yorkers in search of soul food, a cuisine developed by the African-American community in the Southern states, should head for the South Bronx, while those wishing to eat Italian won't go far wrong on Arthur Avenue. The best fresh seafood is served in the City Island area, however. The rest of the neighborhood is a menu of food from all over the world: African, South American, Asian, and anything else you can imagine.

QUEENS

The most popular neighborhood in Queens is Astoria, once known as Greek Town. There are still plenty of Greek bars and restaurants, but there are also lots of other options.

Many young professionals have chosen to move here, attracted by its proximity to Manhattan (the last subway station in Astoria is just ten stops down the line from Times Square), the wide range of bars and restaurants, and the many parks.

One of Astoria's attractions is its beer gardens, open-air spaces where you can smoke and drink, usually close to a brewery or large beer hall. The Bohemian Hall and Beer Garden (2919 24th Avenue) is the only authentic example left in New York and is recommended both for young people looking for a good time and families with kids who want to enjoy an outdoor barbecue (with the adults drinking some good beer). Do note that alcohol on the street is not permitted in New York!

The cannoli at the Italian La Guli Pastry Shop at 29-15 Ditmars Blvd are renowned throughout the city and plenty of New Yorkers come all the way to Queens just to sample them.

Long Island City in Queens is just a subway stop away from Manhattan. The once mainly industrial and manufacturing neighborhood has changed significantly in recent years, with a host of art galleries opening their doors right across the area. The MoMA PS1 contemporary art institution, a subsidiary of the more famous MoMA in Manhattan, is definitely worth a visit.

STATEN ISLAND

This neighborhood is completely different from the rest of NYC. The scenery is more rural and you will see Victorian-style villas and lots of green spaces instead of the city's usual skyscrapers. People from other boroughs don't come here as often and many of the residents are Italian Americans.

Joe Scaravella (owner)

Nonna Adelina (from Naples)

Nonna Maria (from Avellina)

One of the most famous restaurants on Staten Island is Enoteca Maria (27 Hyatt Street), where the cooks aren't professional chefs but a roster of real *nonnas* (grandmothers), who change the menu from week to week.

One of the main draws to Staten Island is the splendid view of Lady Liberty, as the Statue of Liberty is known, and over Manhattan.

The island boasts a number of parks, such as the Staten Island Greenbelt, a system of contiguous parkland that is also one of the areas of greatest biodiversity in New York. You'll also find the Fresh Kills Landfill, which until 2011 was the largest urban landfill in the world, but is now being converted into a park and a habitat for a range of wild animals, a project to be completed by 2037. Staten Island has become a perfect place for lovers of tranquility and nature.

THE CATSKILL MOUNTAINS

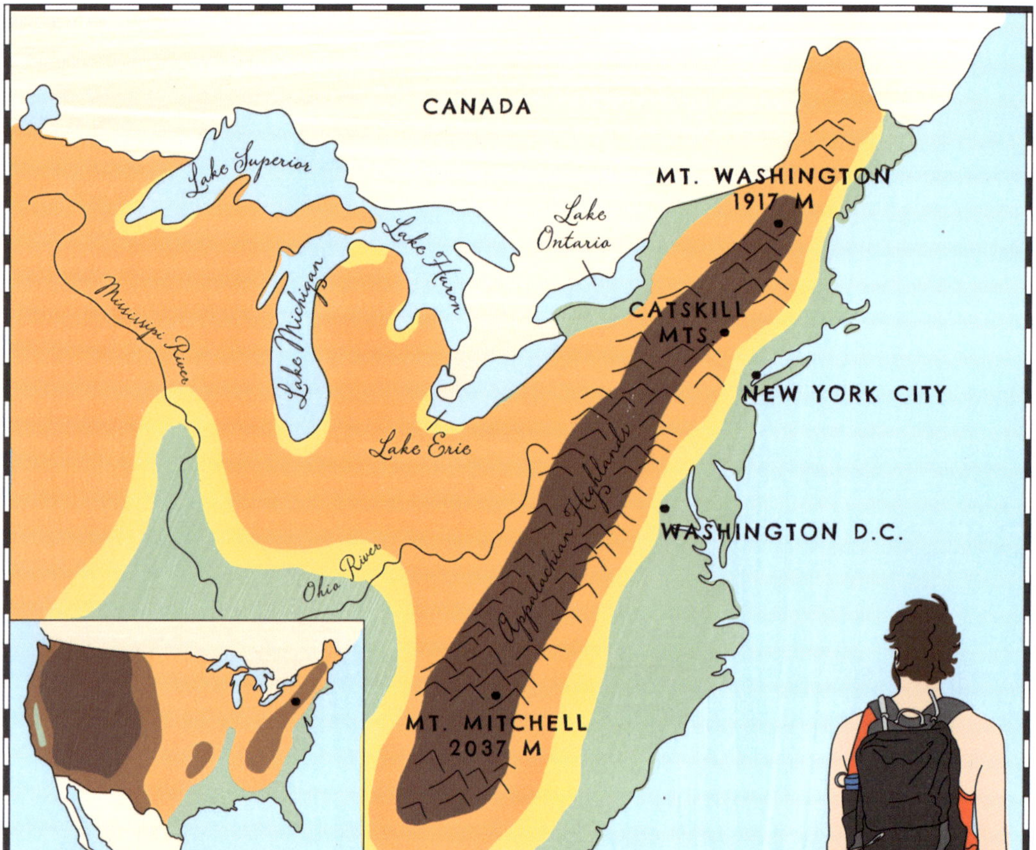

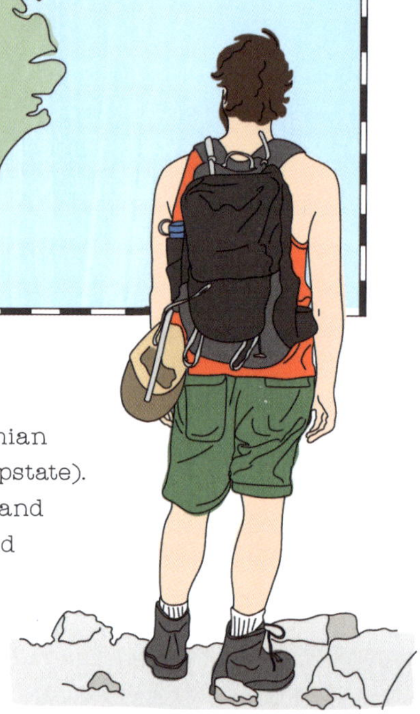

The Catskill Mountains are a subrange of the Appalachian Mountains in the northern part of New York State (aka Upstate). The area is popular with winter sports fans for skiing and snowboarding, and is the perfect place for hiking and rafting in summer.

A recent trend among New Yorkers is glamping—camping that is both eco-friendly and glamorous. You can even rent pre-erected tents furnished with designer furniture.

One example is the geodesic Large Dome, tucked into the woods. The Outlier Inn in Sullivan County is about 90 miles (140 km) outside of New York and you can spend the night in the spectacular transparent geodesic shelter of the Large Dome, combining a love of nature with home comforts.

There are plenty of hiking options for all levels of experience. One of the most beautiful and, fortunately, easiest trails is not far from the Kaaterskill Falls, where a stroll of just over a mile (less than 2 km) will take you to the base of the highest falls in the state.

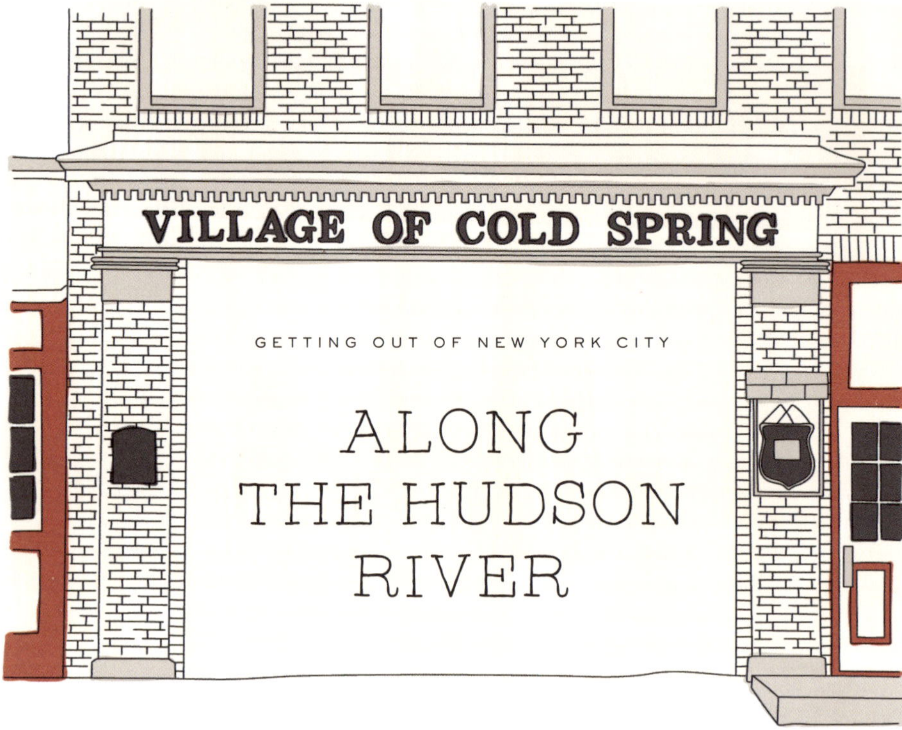

GETTING OUT OF NEW YORK CITY

ALONG THE HUDSON RIVER

Cold Spring

This fascinating historic village, about 60 miles (100 km) from New York, is nestled in the charming Hudson Highlands, which may seem rather familiar to fans of American television series as the views and scenery have featured so often on screen. You will find classic mom-and-pop stores, and even a few lemonade stands, which begin to pop up as spring approaches. This is the ideal place to escape the chaos of the city and experience a slice of real America.

A married couple of art collectors opened Magazzino Italian Art, a museum dedicated to postwar and contemporary Italian art, in Cold Spring in 2017.

Kingston

This small town, 93 miles (150 km) outside of New York City, is a recommended stop for history buffs. One of the oldest districts boasts an area called Four Corners, the only place in the United States where all four buildings on each side of an intersection, at Crown Street and John Street, are built of stone and date back to the pre-Revolutionary period.

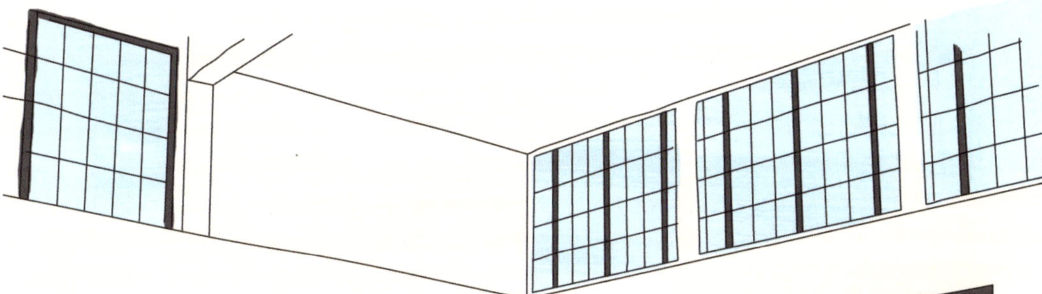

Dia:Beacon

The Dia Art Foundation has been hosting projects and putting on art exhibitions in Beacon, a historic village just up the river, since the 1960s. This led to the opening of an extraordinary museum in the 2000s that now hosts exhibitions of mostly contemporary artists.

Notable artists featured include Louise Bourgeois and Gerhard Richter.

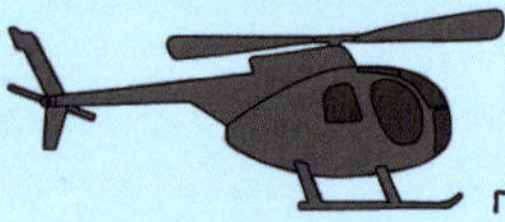

THE HAMPTONS & LONG ISLAND

Long Island is the tongue of land to the east of Manhattan that also includes parts of Brooklyn and Queens. Head even farther out, however, and you will find other destinations much beloved of New Yorkers for weekend expeditions or longer summer stays to enjoy the beaches and delights of the Atlantic Ocean.

The Hamptons is the name New Yorkers give to the easternmost part of Long Island, which has become famous for areas like East Hampton and Southampton. Don't expect beautiful views or the feel of sand between your toes, however. You can sunbathe by the pool and drink chilled champagne, but if you want to take a walk on the beach, you will find many of these are reserved for the exclusive use of the ultra-luxurious villas.

COOPER'S BEACH

Cooper's Beach in Southampton is definitely worth a trip. It was rated one of the best in the United States in 2025.

The Hamptons are relatively easy to get to. It's a three-hour drive or two to three hours on the train from Penn Station. The easiest option of all is the Hampton Jitney, however, a coach service departing from Manhattan that makes several stops and even has free onboard Wi-Fi (hamptonjitney.com).

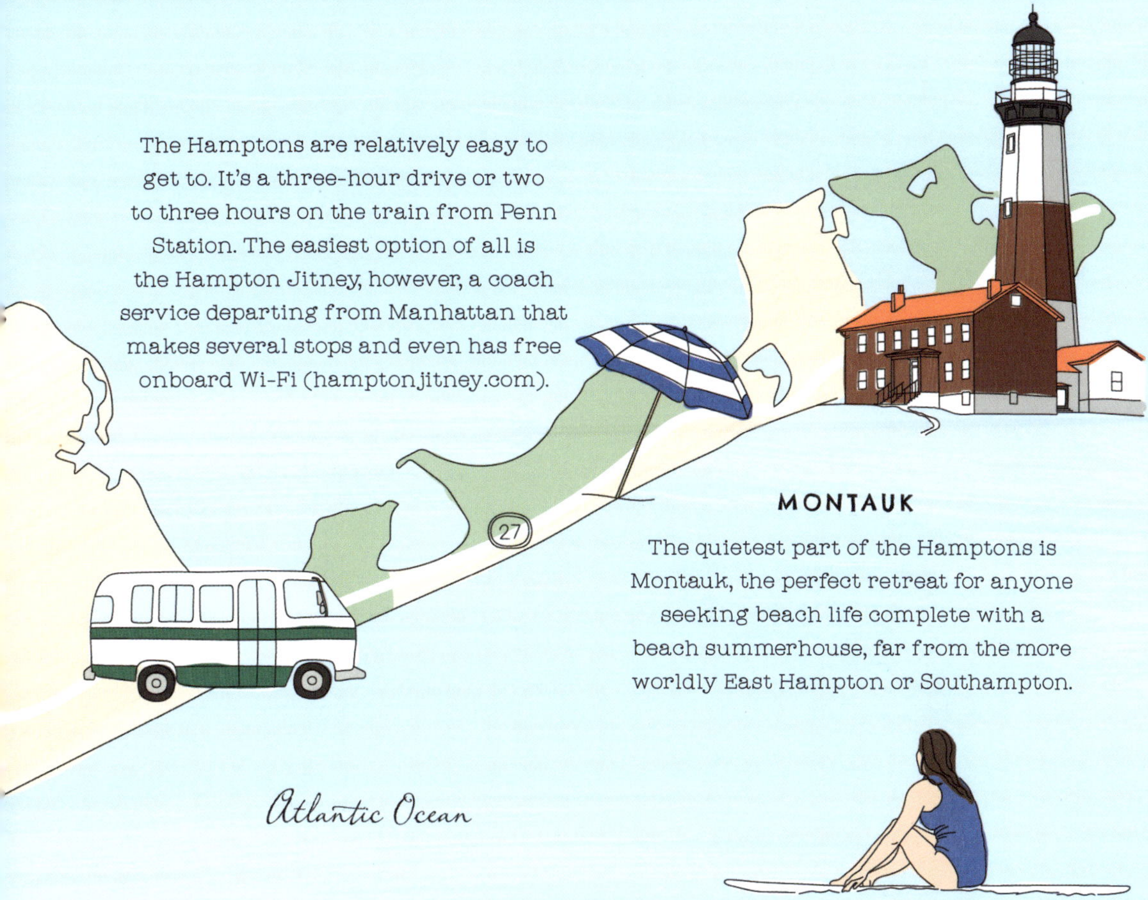

MONTAUK

The quietest part of the Hamptons is Montauk, the perfect retreat for anyone seeking beach life complete with a beach summerhouse, far from the more worldly East Hampton or Southampton.

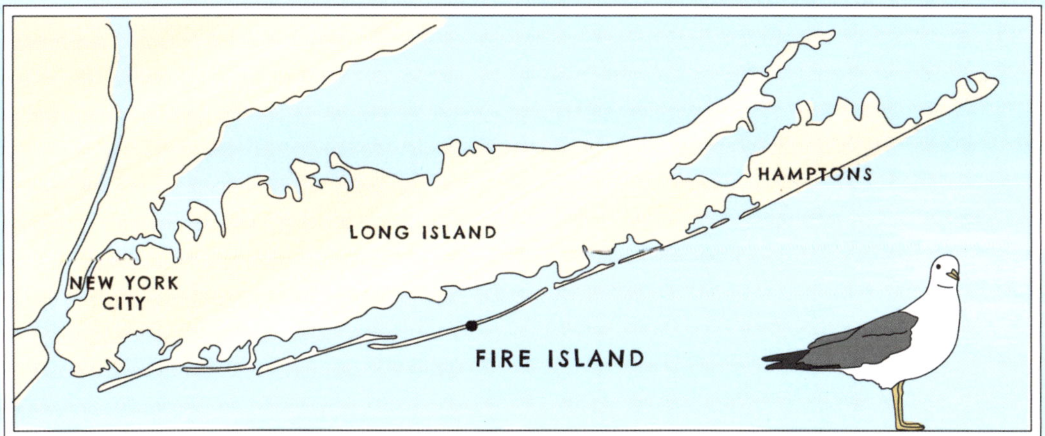

Fire Island is another popular destination. This narrow ribbon of sand and dunes, about 30 miles (50 km) long, runs along the southern coast of the island and is served by little ferries that sail from Long Island across crystal-clear lagoons. The beaches here are open to the public and dotted with small summer hamlets where you can rent a room, as long you book well in advance of the season, of course.

INSTAGRAMMABLE FOOD

New, healthy, and (who would have thought it?) highly colorful foods that are extremely Insta-friendly are popping up like mushrooms wherever you look. It is the same almost everywhere in the world, but the phenomenon is more common in New York than anywhere else.

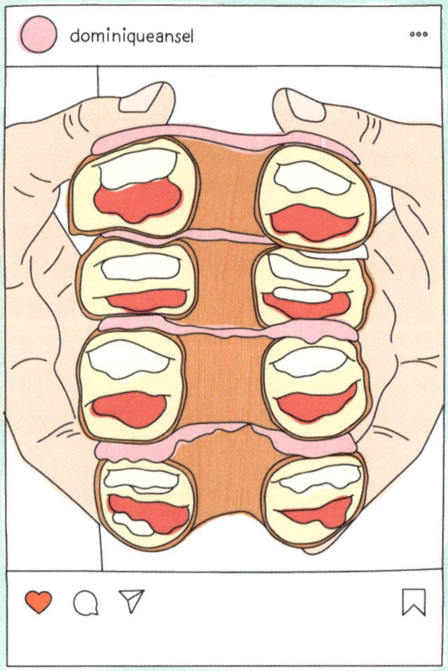

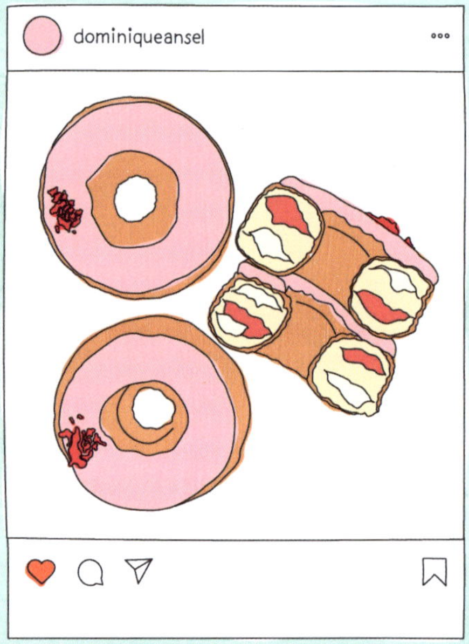

Sweet treats

Phenomena like the cronut (a cross between a croissant and a donut) and the queues to buy them became so famous they even cropped up as a storyline in the popular sitcom *2 Broke Girls*. Treats like crookies (croissants filled with chocolate chip dough), cinnamon rolls, and mochi donut are all the rage now.

A classic place to get your hands on a cronut is the Dominique Ansel Bakery in SoHo (189 Spring Street).

New York once simply couldn't do without ... dishes covered in gold.

A few years ago, there was a craze for chicken wings coated with 24-carat gold dust, which you could buy at various outlets of the Ainsworth restaurant. Prices started at $30 for ten wings, rising to $1,000 for a tray of fifty and a bottle of champagne.

If you want to feel like King Midas.

People are currently also going mad for bubble tea (or boba), a drink of iced tea and tapioca pearls that originated in Taiwan in the 1980s. Patrol the streets of Manhattan toting one of these outsize beakers and you will pass for a true New Yorker.

WORLD CUISINE

Dining out

For real food lovers, the only New York restaurant guide that mattered was *Zagat*, the legendary paperback with a burgundy cover that emerged in the late 1970s when a married couple of lawyers started asking their friends for tips on where they could get a decent meal. The information is now available online at the Infatuation (owned by JP Morgan Chase).

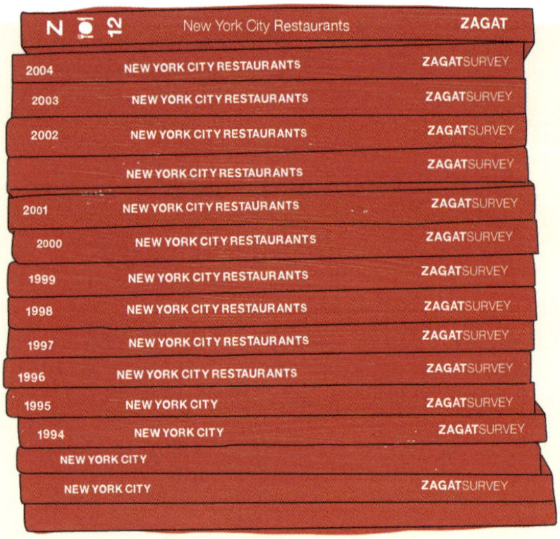

The Infatuation

Although Zagat is no more, the reviews are constantly updated on the highly reliable website (theinfatuation.com) where restaurants are rated by quality, types of cuisine, and neighborhood, so you will always know which places near you are the best for Chinese or Russian food, the trendiest, the most child-friendly, and so on.

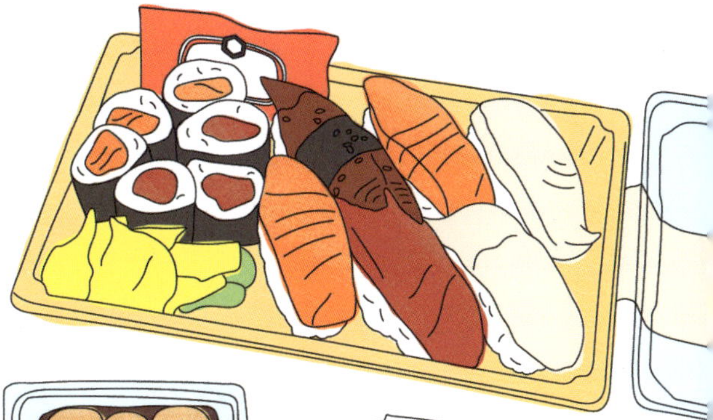

Dining in

If you want to sample the many exotic cuisines the city has to offer and cook them in the comfort of your own home, there is a whole host of delicatessens, grocery stores, and specialist mini-marts to explore. You can buy all the ingredients required for perfect sashimi at Katagiri (224 East 59th Street), the oldest Japanese grocery store in the United States, which has been open since 1907. In addition to freshly prepared fish and sushi, you will also find the best Kobe beef, a Japanese specialty.

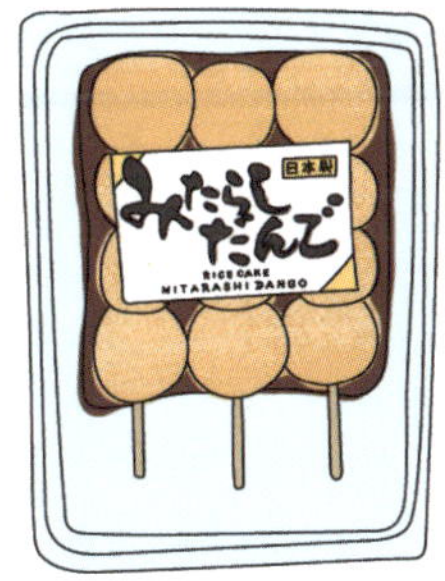

If you crave hot dogs and pancetta, Schaller & Weber (1654 Second Avenue, on the corner of 86th Street) have been selling top-quality German and Central European delicacies since 1937. The best Central American grocery stores are in the Corona neighborhood in Queens, but if you want Polish food, you can't go wrong with an excursion to Greenpoint in Brooklyn.

Penchant for Italian food?

Eataly can help out. It has two branches in Manhattan, one in Midtown at 200 Fifth Avenue and one Downtown at 4 World Trade Center.

BRUNCH: AN OBSESSION

BLOODY MARY

1½ fl oz (45 ml) vodka
3 fl oz (90 ml) tomato juice
1 tbsp (15 ml) lemon juice
3 dashes of Worcestershire sauce
Tabasco, celery salt, pepper

Brunch is an absolute obsession with New Yorkers and a key part of any good start to the weekend. Taking place somewhere between breakfast time and lunchtime, it is an excuse to eat a slightly more substantial first meal of the day with no pangs of guilt since it is also lunch. People generally meet up at about 1.30 P.M. but, bearing in mind that a lot of places don't take reservations, it's best to turn up early.

MIMOSA (BUCK'S FIZZ)

2½ fl oz (75 ml) champagne
2½ fl oz (75 ml) freshly squeezed orange juice

You can forget the taboo about drinking cocktails in the middle of the day at brunch. The classic choice is a Bloody Mary, or alternatively a Mimosa.

Brunch comes in an endless variety of forms, from the most delicate portions at Sarabeth's (40 Central Park South) and the slightly more substantial offerings at The Smith (55 Third Avenue) to the bottomless brunches where you can eat as much as you like for a fixed price. A good place for this is Maya (1191 First Avenue), a Mexican restaurant where you get a two-hour window to order whatever you fancy from a tapas menu.

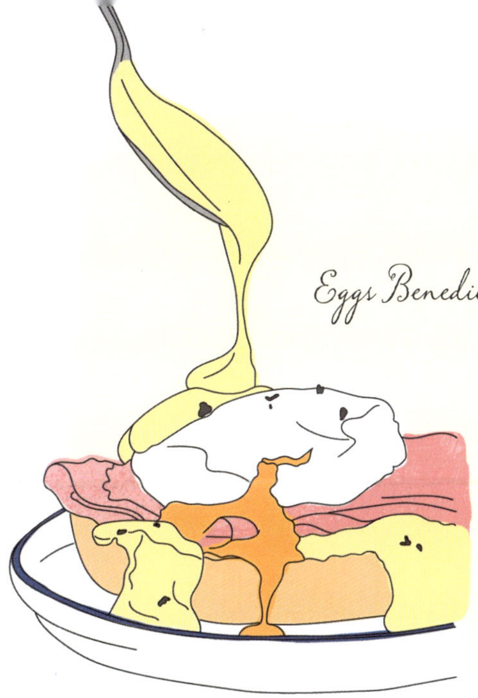

Eggs Benedict

Bagel with lox & cream cheese

The most popular dishes are Eggs Benedict, whose unique selling point is the generous helping of hollandaise sauce, avocado toast, French toast, bagels with lox (smoked salmon) and cream cheese, and of course pancakes. You are very likely to see someone scooping up eggs, pancakes, ketchup, bacon, and maple syrup all in the same forkful. At first, you'll be appalled, but then you'll try it yourself ...

AT THE DINER

Diners are those celebrated restaurants that are open 24/7 where characters in movies go for slap-up breakfasts or late-night suppers. They are pretty much ubiquitous in the city and serve food of every kind.

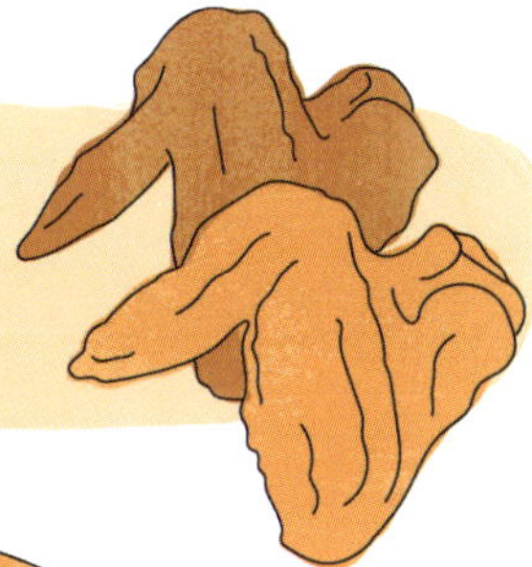

Chicken wings

Onion rings

Bacon pancakes

Banana cream pie

New Yorkers frequent diners mainly for breakfast and you really have to order pancakes, French toast, and eggs done any which way. After a long evening of drinking, choose fries and chicken wings instead.

Salted-caramel pretzel

Options for locals include the Westway Diner (614 Ninth Avenue), which has proclaimed itself the "best diner in Manhattan" and was the place that inspired Jerry Seinfeld and Larry David with the idea for the sitcom *Seinfeld*; the Waverly Diner (385 Sixth Avenue), a Greenwich Village landmark since the 1970s; Zaza (104 Greenwich Street) in the Financial District; and, last but not least, EJ's Luncheonette (1271 Third Avenue) on the Upper East Side where you are sure to find fairly long lines at weekends.

BURGERS

Burgers are to the Americans what pizza is to the Italians. The first thing you need to know is that a real burger is a cheeseburger. Without cheese, you're only getting half the enjoyment. Be aware that every New Yorker is convinced they know the best burger joint in town and will not hesitate to recommend it.

Restaurant chains that do a good-quality burger include:

Bareburger

Uses meat with no preservatives or additives, from bison to the "impossible burger" (vegetarian, but with an "authentic" flavor).

Shake Shack

The menu is less varied here, but their burgers are so tasty, don't be surprised if you feel the need to order another one straight after.

JG Melon

Minetta Tavern

Other places in the city that are real institutions include:

JG Melon (1291 Third Avenue) on the Upper East Side, whose signature dish is crispy circular cottage fries (Note: Takes cash only).

Minetta Tavern (113 MacDougal Street), whose prices are slightly higher, but they have the best meat in town.

Smashed NYC

If the smashed burger is the dish on everybody's lips in New York, this is mostly thanks to Smashed NYC (55 Water Street, Brooklyn), which has perfected the art, turning them out crispy on the outside and juicy within. Every burger is freshly grilled, with homemade sauces and vegan options for an irresistibly delicious experience.

SPRING

New York in the spring usually boasts temperatures that are mild but not yet muggy.

The city fills up with a host of interesting individuals attending the various events held at this time of year, and so is ideal for people-watching, a New Yorker's favorite hobby. This is the season for the biggest art fairs, such as Frieze, which is held in Randall's Island Park on the eponymous islet in the middle of the East River. The island is usually quite difficult to get to, so take advantage of the fair's ferry service to explore the surrounding area.

There is also the Affordable Art Fair at the Metropolitan Pavilion (125 West 18th Street), where you can buy contemporary works from the USA or farther afield for prices ranging from a few hundred dollars to tens of thousands. A host of events are put on in art galleries, stores, and other venues to accompany each festival, making the city even livelier than usual.

Times Square is emptied of cars for the Summer Solstice and the traffic is replaced by people with yoga mats who take part in a massive group class.

Cymbidium orchids

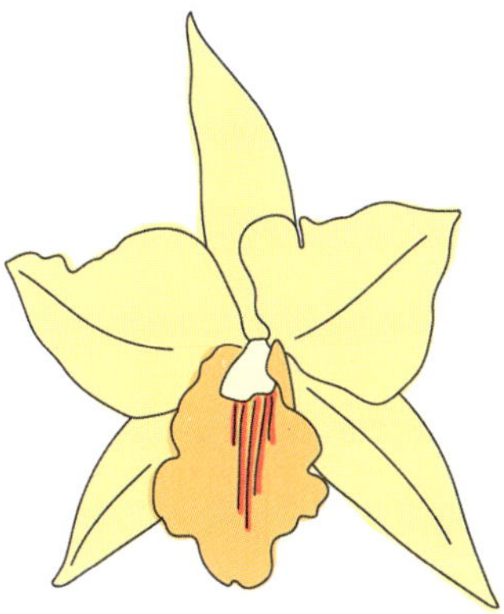

Maxillaria rufescens

Phalaenopsis orchids

Cherry blossom

Brooklyn Botanic Garden is particularly worth a visit when the cherry trees are in blossom (and you can even follow this live on their website), while the New York Botanical Garden in the Bronx puts on an exhibition of rare orchids that attracts both locals and tourists.

SUMMER

New York summers typically feature high temperatures, muggy conditions, humidity, and stinky air.

For all these reasons, people tend to flee the city, and those who have no choice but to stay try to get out on weekends, at least.

Getting out of town

Nearby New Jersey, the Garden State, is one of the most popular destinations, in particular Sandy Hook Beach, the closest to New York. There is even a handy ferry service that will take you there. Embark at the terminal on East 35th Street or Wall Street.

Most of this area is preserved as a National Recreation Area, so you can go on bird-watching trips and even try kitesurfing, if that is your thing.

Staying in town

Nearly every park will screen movies, organize theater performances, or stage gigs, and there will often be free yoga or martial arts classes.

Pinknic

Governors Island sometimes plays host to Pinknic, a music festival awash with rosé wine, at which most of those attending dress up in themed costumes and celebrate the so-called rosé lifestyle.

FALL

The fall is one of the most beautiful seasons to visit New York.

Temperatures are mild and the city is lively but not overrun. You can still get into parks and rooftop bars and enjoy seeing the colors of nature as the foliage changes from gold to copper in fall, a natural phenomenon and very popular with visitors.

Halloween is the festival that people enjoy most during this period, and it is celebrated in America rather differently than in Europe. Imagine a kind of carnival where everyone dresses up however they like. New Yorkers flock to the annual Village Halloween Parade, the biggest in the world, so if you happen to come across it, just join in. It will be a unique experience.

Apple-picking and pumpkin harvest

New Yorkers often migrate to farms upstate during the autumn months to indulge in some of their favorite family activities, such as picking apples to be baked in their famous apple pies ...

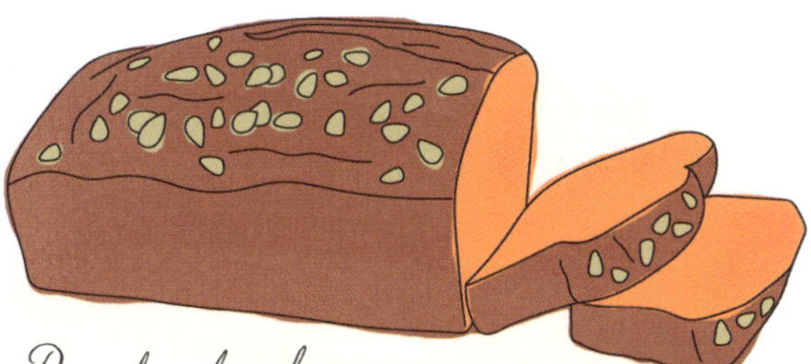

Pumpkin bread

... and to harvest pumpkins, which are used both to decorate their homes and in making confections such as pumpkin bread, a typical American autumnal treat.

WINTER

Winters are unpredictable in New York.

Temperatures can suddenly leap from 40°F to 60°F (5°C to 15°C), only to plummet to 14°F (-10°C) the following day. The wind coming in from the Atlantic also makes the cold feel more intense. The city can feel as if it is almost overflowing in the months of winter, thanks to the visitors drawn in by the many events organized, including the Winter Wonderland and frosty, Christmas-themed parks.

The best-known winter events include the ones in Union Square, Grand Central, and Bryant Park, whose attractions include a free ice rink. As an alternative, the Standard High Line Hotel (848 Washington Street) erects a kind of Alpine winter village, as does Eataly on its rooftop, perfect if you fancy a hot chocolate and some apple pie with cream.

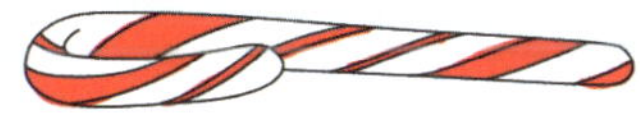

Traditional Christmas shows include the Rockettes' Radio City Spectacular and The Nutcracker.

If you want to see something a little different, however, go for *Kwanzaa*, a dance show put on at the Apollo Theater to celebrate the African-American rights movement in the United States.

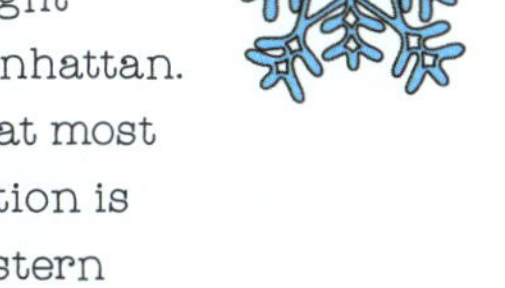

The famous Christmas light displays are not limited to Manhattan. One of the neighborhoods that most famously upholds the tradition is Dyker Heights in southwestern Brooklyn, so be sure to go if you want to dive into a real fairytale.

FOURTH OF JULY

America's Independence Day dates back to 1776 and is celebrated with intense enthusiasm and emotion. The Americans are known for their strong patriotic sentiment. Typical ways of enjoying the day include organizing a family picnic or barbecue followed by a traditional firework display.

The majority of the bars and restaurants in New York stay open, but lots of stores and museums are closed. It is a federal holiday, after all.

The most spectacular firework displays are put on by Macy's, the big department store, and they are launched from an area near the Brooklyn Bridge on the East River.

Lots of New Yorkers choose to reserve a front-row seat in one of the parks in Dumbo (Down Under the Manhattan Bridge Overpass) in order to enjoy the show without having to pay over the odds for orders at local bars and restaurants.

THANKSGIVING

Thanksgiving Day is celebrated on the fourth Thursday in November every year.

The first Thanksgiving was held in Plymouth, Massachusetts, in 1621, when the Pilgrim Fathers gave thanks for a good harvest after a particularly difficult year.

The tradition for Thanksgiving is to gather your family together or, more often, your friends, as the families of most New Yorkers live far away. Festivities revolve around a very heavy meal traditionally consisting of roast turkey, sweet potatoes, wild rice, and gravy, a sauce made with the cooking juices from the turkey, which is often poured over the stuffing, the traditional filling for the turkey.

Gravy

Wild rice

Sweet potatoes

The Macy's Thanksgiving Day Parade is the most spectacular celebration, and is broadcast on live television right across the United States. Be sure not to miss it if you happen to find yourself in New York on this special day and then go and take a seat at a diner, where you'll find the traditional menu on offer.

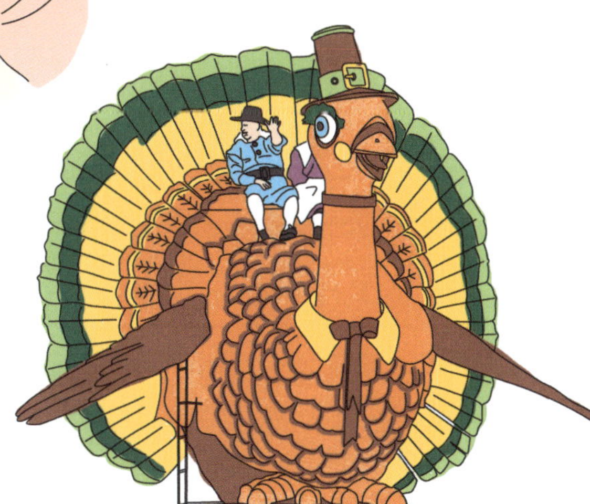

SAINT PATRICK'S DAY

Saint Patrick's Day is on March 17, and it divides New Yorkers into two camps: those who hole up at home to avoid the chaos, and those who love it and can't wait to get out onto the streets to experience it.

Saint Patrick is the patron saint of Ireland, and the Irish community has historically always been a big part of New York.

Many Irish people are religious and some also like to enjoy a drink or two on special occasions, so the day has turned into a rather boozy celebration over the years.

On the evening of Paddy's Day, especially in neighborhoods like the Village, the Meatpacking District, and the Lower East Side, you will see hordes of people out on the streets. They wear string-light necklaces and green clothes and paint their faces, crowding into pubs and breweries as they pay homage to the saint so revered by their ancestors.

NEW YEAR

Mention New Year in New York and you immediately think of Times Square and the iconic dropping of the glowing sphere with crystals and LED lights. New Yorkers tend to do all they can to avoid it.

Instead, locals prefer to spend this special night at a private party or a bash organized in one of the city's many clubs. Some will even try to find a nice rooftop from which to enjoy a view of the firework display in privacy.

You are advised to avoid heroics and wrap up warm, as it is usually a particularly cold night.

Try to resist the temptations of the many party options on offer. Traveling between celebrations risks getting stuck in traffic and you may end up celebrating the arrival of midnight out on the street somewhere.

A YEAR IN NEW YORK

CHINESE NEW YEAR

New Year festivities don't fizzle out on January 1 in New York. Celebrations continue into the Chinese New Year, marked by both the Chinese community and many other city dwellers who need no excuse to party.

The Chinese Lunar New Year is a movable feast, falling between January 21 and February 19 each year and celebrated with a big parade through Chinatown that features traditional, colorful dragons, red lanterns, and dancers in traditional dress, while the top restaurants sell street food to mark the occasion. During this period, places like Flushing Town Hall (137–35 Northern Blvd) put on performances of traditional Chinese culture that are always fascinating to watch.

A Wishing Tree is also set up on Madison Avenue between 62nd and 64th Streets, where anyone can write a wish for the coming year, place it in a traditional red envelope, and hang it on the tree.

TRAVEL NOTES

TRAVEL NOTES

TRAVEL NOTES

TRAVEL NOTES

TRAVEL NOTES

TRAVEL NOTES

TRAVEL NOTES

TRAVEL NOTES

TO DO LIST

TO DO LIST

THE AUTHORS

The late Elisabetta Cirillo was born in Brescia on August 1, 1986, and graduated with a degree in modern languages from the Catholic University of the same city. Thanks to her studies and her family circumstances, she traveled extensively from childhood, living in New Zealand, South Africa, Moscow, and New York, where she discovered a passion for yoga. She had a special relationship with the United States, and the American way of thinking and living soaked into her mindset, influencing her choices and attitudes. She opened her Yoga Shala Sadhana studio in Brescia's Le Tre Torri multifunctional center in 2014 and, in 2016, published the poetry collection *Fino a qui* (Rubettino Editore). Her first novel *Come capita la vita* (Sperling & Kupfer) appeared in 2019.

Monica Lovati began her career with Massimo Pitis, concentrating on visual identity and editorial design projects. She had the privilege of working with the late Ettore Sottsass, under whose artistic direction she learned a new creative approach that has influenced her thinking and vision. She went on to work as an art director for Mario Milizia's studio in the worlds of fashion and luxury goods. In 2010, she opened her own studio specializing in artistic direction, visual identity, and illustration.

The author and the publisher would like to thank Marco Ausenda and Laura Pezzino for their invaluable help in creating this book.

Originally published in 2019 by Mondadori Electa S.p.A., Milano
for Libri Illustrati Rizzoli

First published in English in 2026
by Rizzoli Universe, a division of
Rizzoli International Publications

Rizzoli International Publications Inc
49 West 27th Street
New York, NY 10001

Rizzoli International Publications UK Ltd
Somerset House, West Wing
Strand, London WC2R 1LA

www.rizzoliusa.com

Publisher: Charles Miers
Associate Publisher: Tina Persaud
Senior Editor: Kristy Richardson
Graphic design and illustrations: Monica Lovati

 A CIP catalogue record for this book is available from the British Library.

ISBN 9780789346872

2026 / 1
Printed in Italy

The authorized representative in the EU for safety and compliance is Mondadori Libri S.p.A., via Gian Battista Vico 42, Milan, Italy, 0123, www.mondadori.it

Visit us online: Instagram.com/RizzoliBooks
Facebook.com/RizzoliNewYork
Youtube.com/user/RizzoliNY

PEFC Certified
This product is from sustainably managed forests and controlled sources
PEFC/18-31-1413
www.pefc.org